Medieval Academy Reprints fc

Medieval Academy Reprints for Teaching

John B. Morrall

POLITICAL THOUGHT
IN MEDIEVAL TIMES

Published by University of Toronto Press
Toronto Buffalo London
in association with the Medieval Academy of America

© Medieval Academy of America 1980
Printed in Canada
ISBN 0-8020-6413-2
reprinted 1987, 1989, 1994, 1997

First published by Hutchinson & Co Ltd, London,
in 1958. This edition reprinted from the 1962 Harper
Torchbook by arrangement with Harper & Row, Publishers,
Incorporated. The illustration on the front cover, Frederick
Barbarossa as a crusader, is a detail of folio 1^r, ms Vat
lat 2001, reproduced with the permission of the Biblioteca
Apostolica Vaticana.

Canadian Cataloguing in Publication Data

Morrall, John B.
  Political thought in medieval times

  (Medieval Academy reprints for teaching ; 7)
  Includes bibliographical references and index.
  ISBN 0-8020-6413-2

  1. Political science – Europe – History.
  2. Europe – Politics and government – 476–1492.
  I. Medieval Academy of America. II. Title.
  III. Series.

JA82.M67 1994   320.902   C94-931528-1

CONTENTS

AUTHOR'S NOTE

The great extent to which I stand in debt to modern experts on the various aspects of this subject will be at once obvious from a glance at the bibliography. It has not always been possible to acknowledge in its proper place in the text the picking of this brain or the choosing of that idea, but here and now I would like to say how much I have in general benefited from the work of previous writers on the subject; indeed one of the aims of this little book is to introduce the interested reader to some of the results of their work and to some of the problems arising from it.

To one authority mentioned, Sir Maurice Powicke, I owe a particularly personal debt. Sir Maurice's help in the writing of this book has been far more than merely editorial. His critical advice, forthright but constructive, has been available to me at every stage and there must be few pages of the book which have not profited from it. It should hardly be necessary to add that whatever defects remain in the book (and there must be many) are not Sir Maurice's responsibility but my own.

My wife has acted as a guinea pig by reading the various drafts of this book from the standpoint of the non-specialist reader, with a general interest in history and political thought, for whom it is intended. I owe to her especial thanks for detecting and helping to eliminate the all too easy intrusion of technical obscurity, allusiveness and jargon.

I would finally like also to mention my gratitude to my parents, who first gave me the opportunity and encouragement to embark on the study of history, and to my brother, with whom as a boy I shared an initial interest in the Middle Ages.

J. B. M.

CHAPTER I

WHAT WAS 'MEDIEVAL' POLITICAL THOUGHT?

THE western European world of the Middle Ages originated from a death—that of the old Roman Empire of classical antiquity. For long this formidable institution had provided a workable social and political unity for the lands of the Mediterranean basin and their hinterlands. But in the fourth and fifth centuries A.D. the whole existing structure of Roman civilization in the western part of this area collapsed before what Gibbon in the eighteenth century was to describe as 'the triumph of barbarism and Christianity', and what Arnold Toynbee in the twentieth was to call the pressure of the external and internal proletariats. Both writers mean much the same thing beneath their differences of terminology and both would seem to be right.

The successful challenge to pagan Rome—by the barbarians in the sphere of temporal force and by Christianity in the sphere of dynamic spiritual vitality—spelt the failure of the whole Graeco-Roman cultural tradition in its self-appointed task of building a durable political society on purely rational foundations, with an appropriate backing of material force. The attempt to shore up this faltering Leviathan with synthetic religious feeling centering on the cult of Rome and the Emperor was ultimately useless.

In the east at Constantinople the Byzantine successors of Constantine followed their founder's example by frank cooperation with the new spiritual force of Christianity, in return for a large measure of control over it; the result was that toughly durable politico-religious organism, the Byzantine Empire, which preserved the old classical ideal of a strong centralized political unit based on a commonly accepted law and government. The Byzantine Church supplied the Empire with the cohesive ideological force which it needed if it was to avoid the disintegration which had overtaken its Roman predecessor in the west. But despite the paramount role played by Christianity in Byzantine civilization, it is not unfair to say that Christian Byzantium was in the same line of development as the monarchies and city states of pagan antiquity, where a religious tradition served as the apotheosis and sanctification of political society's norms of authority and power.

In the apparently less fortunate western half of the Roman Empire a completely different development ultimately emerged. There the Germanic invaders changed the whole political compound in decisive fashion by introducing quite a new element—personal and tribal custom, which acted as a dissolving force on any remaining idea of a centralized governmental political framework. The State as we should understand it today did not exist in the barbarian dark ages. Christianity alone was left with the task of providing the west with a social unity across its new barbarian frontiers. It did so by appealing not to a primarily political sense of obligation, but to a basis of divinely inspired and commonly shared spiritual fellowship. Medieval Europe offers for the first time in history the somewhat paradoxical spectacle of a society trying to organize itself politically on the basis of a spiritual framework (which gives to political life merely a relative value). By so doing western European thought about politics was propelled along lines which were to be sharply different from those of any other human society.

We may now attempt a definition of that unsatisfactory but irreplaceable term, the Middle Ages. It may be taken to mean, for our present purpose, the broad period within which the classical world's approach to the problem of political life was reversed, 'stood on its head', as Marx would have put it. Instead of religion, as hitherto, forming the buttress for a communal political tradition, it was now elevated essentially above the political sphere and from this position of transcendence it bestowed on political authority whatever limited justification the latter possessed. This fundamental dependence of society on a religious faith which it is assumed that all true citizens must share makes it legitimate to describe medieval society as a Christian Commonwealth. Conversely the disappearance in practice and finally also in theory of this dependence may be taken as marking the end of the medieval period of western European history. The Reformation, whatever view may be taken of it theologically, marks the point beyond which a visible and permanent religious conflict finally ended the medieval struggle to organize the whole of western Christendom on the basis of a universally accepted interpretation of Christianity.

The chronological limits of this book are therefore provided by the fall of the Graeco-Roman civilization in the west on the one hand and by the Reformation on the other. The central theme of the book will, it is hoped, emerge as the rise, development and collapse of the ideal of a Christian Commonwealth and its replacement by a return to a more purely political conception of the State. To what extent fundamental ideas inspired by the Commonwealth remain in disguise in modern notions of the State is not for us to determine here. Our task is rather to enquire what political thought meant for men of the Middle Ages, for it is only by asking this question that we can hope for even a remote insight into this thought in its living historical background.

CHAPTER II

CHURCH, EMPIRE AND BARBARIANS

JUST as the racial composition of medieval Europe was the product of a mixture of Germanic and Latin elements, so its political ideals resulted from the marriage of the same two forces, sanctified by the Catholic Western Church. What did each of these three factors, Church, Empire and barbarians, bring to the fusion?

All our knowledge of the social structures of the Germanic invaders is based on written evidence deriving from periods much later than the invasions and settlements in the lands of the Roman Empire. Hence it would be foolish to make dogmatic deductions about the life of the German tribes before their incursions across the imperial borders. It is true that we have statements from Latin writers such as Caesar and Tacitus, purporting to give descriptions of the contemporary life of these barbarians in the first centuries B.C. and A.D. But these accounts need more corroboration before they can be taken at their face value. It is safer to admit frankly that we can know little about the primitive phases of Germanic history and to concentrate on the more certain evidence provided by later periods when the newcomers were already across the threshold of the Roman world.

The new Teutonic kingdoms in the west were formed by the domination of a minority of military conquerors over a Romanized provincial population. In such kingdoms, authority tended to centre in the person of the chieftain who was the warrior leader of the military aristocracy. Such a chieftain or king (as the Anglo-Saxon branch of the Teutonic peoples were to call him) was chosen from a particular family which was thought to possess an inherent right to leadership of the tribe.

12

The original meaning of the Old English word 'cyning', from which our present 'king' derives, is 'a member of the kindred', the family from which the chief was chosen. A rudimentary form of election and acclamation by the assembled warriors was customarily expressed by some such symbolic action as the elevation of the new king on a shield to indicate his assumption of military leadership.

The royal family's monopoly of rule was usually strengthened by a tradition of its divine origin; thus the Frankish Merovingian dynasty traced its ancestry to the seagod Meroveus. Even the acceptance of Christianity did not abolish the sacrosanct aura with which primordial pagan superstition had invested the royal kin. Only with great reluctance would the tribe look for a king outside the royal family. For a good half of the period of Merovingian rule over the Franks the dynasty had no more than nominal power, the practical functions of government being taken over by the so-called 'mayors of the palace', again on a family basis. But the Carolingian mayors did not venture to take the royal title for themselves until fortified in 752 by a more potent religious buttress than paganism could provide—the sanction of the Papacy.

The royal family's claim to the throne was collective. Succession by primogeniture was by no means the rule; only in the more settled conditions of the later medieval centuries did the right of inheriting kingly powers come to be limited primarily to the king's eldest son. In the dark ages it was more necessary that an individual king should be chosen on his merits of seniority, experience or military prowess. To the German successor-kingdoms of the Western Roman Empire, the monarch was not primarily the head of a territorial State but a personal tribal leader; it might not be too wide of the mark to think of him as a gangster chief, surrounded by his henchmen and living with them off the country they had conquered. The Romanized subjects of his conquered territory would be taken under his protection and preserved, in return

13

for concessions in money or in kind, from attacks by other gangster leaders.

The principle of protection in return for service is one of the keys to the complex of personal legal relations so characteristic of medieval society. In an age when material force was the strongest political argument, the practice of protection of the weak by the strong became widespread over western Europe. Not only the king but lesser warriors and nobles were prepared to grant protection on terms favourable to themselves. So arose the custom of commendation of a free man to the protection of a superior, such commendation being accompanied by a promise to perform certain services for the protector. The arrangement might also be applied by the king to provide recompense for his chief fighting men, whose equipment, as the dark ages progressed, became more and more expensive with the development of heavily armed cavalry as the most effective weapon in war.

The services exacted by a superior, whether king or noble, from his protected dependents or vassals came to be of a largely military character, stabilized on a basis of land tenure. Roman legal conceptions had in the late imperial period evolved the notion of the benefice, a form of land tenure granted by the proprietor in return for fixed dues and quasi-permanent services. The dark ages saw the gradual assimilation of the two concepts of vassalage and the benefice; thus personal relationship was linked with land possession.

This assimilation led to the grant or assumption of public political authority by the military landowning elements who now exercized in their localities the administrative and judicial functions regarded in Roman times as the sole prerogative of the central government. This decentralization of political authority in western Europe had its parallel in the decline of economic unity in the Mediterranean basin during the same period, though the economic fragmentation can perhaps be exaggerated. The comparative lessening of trade and commerce and the rise of a predominantly agricultural economy of local

14

units, each self-sufficient for the bare necessities of life, led to a narrowing of mental horizons to the village, the parish or at most the province. Under such conditions political decentralization was natural and inevitable.

Germanic customs of property-holding played its part in this centrifugal process. Teutonic custom, formulated later into feudal law, saw nothing inconsistent in the belief that the same piece of land could be owned by two or more persons, each ownership being in a different sense from the rest. One man might own the land as its absolute overlord, while others might actually use and possess it; each would have his own perfectly good legal claim to the land. Such divided ownership was quite foreign to the more severely logical Roman law, for which a piece of property could possess only one true owner. In this matter modern English law is unique in remaining faithful to its Germanic origins; when the present-day householder grumbles at having to pay his ground rent he might console himself with the reflection that he is helping to continue an extremely venerable tradition.

The Germanic view had even deeper implications. Just as property was shared, so was the law itself, the profoundest expression of tribal communal life. For the Germans, law was something which had existed from time immemorial as a guarantee of the rights of every individual member of the nation which shared the law. It was not necessarily formulated in a written code; indeed unwritten custom was often supposed to have the stronger claim precisely because it was not subject to the human manipulation of writing.

The same spirit led in judicial matters to reliance on what would seem to us the fantastic methods of trial by ordeal or by battle. On solemn occasions or in disputed cases the law might be declared or interpreted by the king in conjunction with his chief advisers; indeed this, with the waging of war, formed the king's essential function. The presence of the body of leading statesmen and nobles who joined the king in thus declaring the law was equally essential. The shadowy figures

15

whose names round off so many Anglo-Saxon and Frankish charters or who are referred to in general terms as giving their assent to royal decisions were undoubtedly considered to be in some undefined way the spokesmen of the whole community. These early royal councils assisted the king in his duties as guardian of the law; he and they had as yet no intention of creating new law. Such an intention would have been, from the point of view of these early medieval times, not only superfluous (for if the law was good, why change it?) but even semi-blasphemous, for the law, like kingship, possessed its own sacrosanct aura. Instead, king and councillors thought of themselves as merely explaining or clarifying the true meaning of the already existing and complete body of law.

Germanic custom handed on to the medieval mind an idea which it never was able to forget, even when in practice it behaved otherwise. This idea was that good laws were rediscovered or restated but never remade. The king and his people both stood under a mutual obligation to preserve the law from infringement or corruption and in some cases when the king clearly failed to do his duty we find his subjects taking matters into their own hands and deposing him. Such drastic action was, however, relatively infrequent. The ingrained reverence of the Germanic peoples for their monarchs was so great that they were prepared to tolerate quite a lot from them. Some modern scholars have spoken of a primitive Germanic theory of the right of resistance of the community to royal misgovernment, but it seems unlikely that any such coherent theory had been formulated at this early period. That move was to come later under the twofold influence of systematized feudal ideas and of the Church's disputes with temporal monarchs. In the famous case of a deposition of Louis the Pious (814–840), Charlemagne's successor, in 833, it is significant that the architects of the whole process were, despite Louis's sobriquet, the bishops of the realm.

The folk-law, being the exclusive property of the tribe, had no pretensions to universality. The barbarian conquerors

16

generally made no attempt to impose a uniform legal code on their new territories. The maxim that every man must be judged by the law of his own people was strictly observed; what was more, he carried round with him, wherever he went, the right to live under his own law. The person rather than the territory was the unit of legal reference. It was common to find many different codes of customary law in force in the same kingdom, town or village, even in the same house, if the ninth-century bishop Agobard of Lyons is to be believed when he says, 'It often happened that five men were present or sitting together, and not one of them had the same law as another.'

An important result of this situation was the continued survival of Roman law, though in debased forms. The majority of the subject populations in the new kingdoms were Latin-speaking provincials of the old Empire. These, in the eyes of their barbarian rulers, would still be Romans and therefore entitled to live under Roman law. Some barbarian kings like the Visigoth Alaric II of Spain (484–507) actually compiled compendia of Roman legal maxims, which served as codes for their kingdoms. The Roman lawyers of the second and third centuries A.D. would have been shocked at this placing of the laws of the Empire on the same footing as those of Teutonic barbarians; but it seems likely that this degradation of Roman law was the condition of its survival in the west.

The deference of the barbarians towards Roman law is an illustration of the glamour which for them still hung round the name of Rome and its imperial past. Even the Anglo-Saxons, who went furthest towards blotting out Roman civilization in the land they conquered, looked on the ruined Roman cities with awe as the work of giants. To the Continental barbarians, whose contact with Roman culture was more immediate and less destructive, the feeling that they held their territories as heirs to the old Empire would be natural. Their coins, their written documents, their buildings and art were all indifferent copies of Roman models. In addition the present reality of that still living Rome called Byzantium, with

17

its absolute Emperor and its luxurious civilization, could not be ignored. In comparison with the *régime* at Constantinople the western countries remained backward children. Here was another factor to keep the memory of Rome alive. No wonder that the highest claim to authority of the Germanic rulers was the fiction that they were deputies for Roman authority, past or present. In the seventh century a bishop in the Visigothic kingdom, St. Isidore of Seville (*d.* 636), made an academic attempt to rationalize the position by arguing that the barbarian states were *Regna* within the framework of the Empire (*Imperium*). This convenient solution was widely accepted. The fact remained, however, that in practice the west was now reorganizing itself on the basis of the territorial kingdom rather than of the universal Empire. Charlemagne's ramshackle Frankish Empire did not modify this process in any permanent sense.

The barbarians were confronted, not only by the dying western Empire but by the far from defunct western Church. This was now organized on the basis of a territorial episcopate over which the Roman Papacy claimed primacy and doctrinal guidance. Before we can assess what contribution the Church made to the still rudimentary medieval political order, we have to look at some of the ideas on political authority which Christian thinkers had formulated as a result of the Church's experiences in its relationship with the Roman Empire in both its pagan and Christian forms.

The early Church had been often persecuted by pagan Emperors because of its refusal to participate in the cult of Emperor-worship, considered by Rome as necessary to cement its hold over the Mediterranean world. Despite this imperial hostility, perhaps indeed because of it, the orthodox Church was always anxious to prove its loyalty to duly constituted political authority, even while pointing out its limits. The same tension between loyalty and resistance persisted in changed terms under the Christian Empire after Constantine, when the danger was not outright persecution but control by

18

the imperial authority in the guise of an arbitrator in doctrinal disputes. Thus the Emperor began to occupy the position (which in Byzantium he never lost) of effective practical head of the Church.

Present-day historians usually describe this attempted combination of temporal and spiritual functions by the term Caesaro-papism, indicating that the Emperor takes upon himself the duties of the Papacy and claims spiritual headship of the Church.

In its effort to preserve its independence the Church emphasized more strongly the relative character of earthly authority. The influence of the dogma of original sin led many of the Church Fathers to conclude that political authority was a consequence of man's corrupted nature, a punishment and at the same time a remedy for his sins. This theory was in opposition to the classical Greek idea, expressed by Plato (427–347 B.C.), and Aristotle (384–322 B.C.), of the natural character of political association and government. Aristotle's maxim that 'Man is a political animal' was forgotten and the origins of political life were held to be conventional, the result of an agreement between imperfect men to make the best of a bad job. Familiar contemporary institutions such as property and slavery were also supposed by the Fathers to have resulted from the fall of man.

These ideas on the conventional character of political authority were not without parallel in pagan sources. The Stoic philosophy, so popular in Rome at the beginning of the Christian era, had in some of its exponents, such as Seneca (*d.* A.D. 65), made the distinction between a golden age of humanity when all men lived in happy equality, not needing to govern or be governed, and the present imperfect age resulting from man's corruption. The only point of difference was that Seneca assigned to civilization the role which Christianity assigned to the devil.

Another Stoic legacy of which Christian thought later made much use was the idea of a universal law of nature, a

19

cosmic principle linking together all living beings and directing them to the proper fulfilment of their respective natures. Neither the Stoic philosophers who propounded the idea nor the Roman lawyers who used it in their jurisprudence were always quite clear whether this natural law was an instinct which man shared with the rest of the animal world or whether it was something peculiar to him, attainable only by the rational power which he alone possessed. Christian writers in the dark ages tended to choose the second alternative, which had some resemblance to the New Testament doctrine of the individual conscience present in each human person. The Roman lawyers' further classification of law into *ius gentium* (general human deductions from or additions to the natural law) and *ius civile* (legal enactments made by separate political entities) were also taken over and reinterpreted. Thus the *ius gentium*, thought of in legal theory as embodying institutions like slavery and property which derogated from the original equality enjoyed by all men under natural law, was often associated by the Christian Fathers with the conditions of life imposed on man after the fall.

The changed attitudes to political thought brought about by early Christianity is most strikingly illustrated in the writings of St. Augustine of Hippo (354–430). Augustine's whole theology is an extended commentary on the antithesis between the redeemed Christian soul, predestined to salvation, and the corrupt fallen society of unredeemed mankind, 'the mass of perdition', as he often unflatteringly calls it. The stark contrast which Augustine made here influenced his comments on politics in his long treatise, *The City of God* (written between 413 and 427).

Civitas Dei is not primarily intended as a work on political philosophy but as a general vindication of the Christian religion against pagan critics who saw it as responsible for the collapse of the Roman Empire in Augustine's own lifetime. In replying discursively to their various charges Augustine builds up what is in effect the first systematic attempt at a Christian

20

philosophy of history. His book depicts the whole story of mankind, past, present and future, in terms of the antagonism between two cities, the city of God and the city of the devil. Augustine nowhere actually identifies the Church with the city of God or the State with the city of the devil; his theology held that elect and reprobate would be inextricably mixed in both institutions until the Last Judgement.

The problem of the relationship of the Christian to existing earthly political authority is dealt with by Augustine in Book XIX of his treatise. He argues that true justice cannot exist in a pagan State which denies God his due of worship and obedience. Only a Christian political community can be a true commonwealth, i.e. one which fully implements the indispensable requirement of justice. Augustine therefore denies the title of *Respublica* (Commonwealth) to a non-Christian political community, though he concedes that it could be considered as a State of a kind if its citizens had a common aim, even if that aim could not be justice itself. Such a State could provide a minimum basis of material order and tranquillity which Christians within it could use during their earthly pilgrimage.

It is clear that, whether the State is Christian or non-Christian, it occupies for Augustine a much humbler position than it had for classical antiquity. Originating, like the Roman Empire itself, from the aggressive desire of fallen men to dominate their fellows, its *raison d'être* in the providential designs of God is to act as a curb to the excesses of a sinful humanity and, at the best, to make the world safe for Christianity by co-operating wholeheartedly with the Church. Of course it could only do so by being itself submissive to orthodox Catholic Christianity and Augustine paints a rosy picture elsewhere in the *City of God* of the virtues of Christian emperors such as Constantine and Theodosius.

His own troubles as a bishop with heretics in North Africa led Augustine to believe in the rightness of coercive pressure by the orthodox State against heretics or schismatics at the bidding of the Church. The theory of material punishment of spiritual error was to be a commonly accepted social principle of medieval Europe.

The Christianization of the Empire, which was being brought about as Augustine wrote, and the subsequent conversion of the barbarian races resulted ultimately in a conception of Europe as being one Church-State or Christendom, as it came to be called in the ninth century. Inside this Christian framework there were divisions of functions between, on the one hand, the ecclesiastical clerical hierarchy (the *Sacerdotium*) and, on the other, the secular rulers, whether Empire (*Imperium*) or kingdom (*Regnum*).

These two broad divisions, corresponding respectively to man's spiritual and temporal needs, shared the government of the Christian world. Both possessed valid grounds of jurisdiction in a Christian society and should in theory have formed harmoniously complementary parts of Augustine's ideally just political and social system. In practice there were frequent clashes between the two authorities because the sphere of influence of either was still insufficiently delimited.

At the end of the fifth century Pope Gelasius I (492–496) tried to mark out a clearer frontier when he wrote to the Byzantine Emperor Anastasius I (491–518), in a famous letter, that 'the two powers by which this world is chiefly ruled' were 'the sacred authority (*auctoritas*) of the Popes and the royal power (*potestas*)'. Gelasius, chiefly concerned to rebut the Emperor's attempt to regulate the Church's doctrinal affairs, added that the spiritual power was comparatively the higher of the two, being in charge of the souls of men, including those of rulers themselves. His use of the Roman legal terms *auctoritas* and *potestas* (indicating respectively the ultimate sovereign source of government and the delegated executive agency which exercises government) was probably intended to emphasize the superiority of the spiritual power on such a comparative assessment.

There seems no need to read into this letter an assertion

22

of papal supremacy over the Empire in the latter's own temporal sphere. Such an interpretation would square neither with the words of Gelasius himself, who admits that 'in matters pertaining to the administration of public discipline the bishops of the Church . . . are themselves obedient' to imperial law, nor with the behaviour and language of later Popes of the dark ages. Many of these, including St. Gregory the Great (590–604), showed an almost servile respect for the imperial authority.

The criticism that could justifiably be made of the Gelasian definition is not that it claimed too much but that it was too ambiguous. It stated quite firmly that there was a border between the two authorities but what it did not make clear was where the border was to be drawn. Hence it was to be quoted with equal confidence by apologists of either power in the great medieval conflicts between the two.

Gelasius was writing from an Italy ruled by the Ostrogoth Theodoric (493–526), but he still thought of the problem in terms of the relationship between the Church and the Empire. After the failure of the superficial Byzantine reconquest under Justinian I (527–565) the Church in the west was brought face to face with the multiplicity of the new barbarian kingdoms. In a sense the Church found an advantage in this change of sparring partner.

The new kings and kinglets felt less sure of their independent rights *vis-à-vis* the Church than had the Empire, with its formidable legal tradition behind it. The papacy stood in a special relationship to the newly-converted barbarian kingdoms and its political support was not to be undervalued, as the Franks, conquering Gaul in the name of Catholicism, found. The Church used its privileged position to try to persuade the new rulers of the west, whether Anglo-Saxon, Frank or Visigoth, that the political power they had forcibly acquired should be used for moral and religious purposes. In the seventh century Isidore of Seville spoke of the monarch as using the material force and terror at his disposal to ensure that his subjects follow a Christian way of life.

23

This ideal of royalty found expression in the various ceremonies of anointing, enthronement and coronation which spread to all the western kingdoms during the seventh and eighth centuries. These ceremonies, controlled and performed by the Church hierarchy, incorporated the secular Germanic idea that the king's chief duty was to be guardian of the community's law; in all the rituals the king promised to perform this duty faithfully. But the important thing was that his promise was made to the Church as well as to the secular community of his subjects and was confirmed by a religious oath. By performing the acts of anointing and coronation the Church made the first great step towards claiming the ultimate regulation of secular political authority, especially as the monarch's promises included undertakings to defend the interests of the Church with his material strength.

The Christianization of royal authority was not an unmixed blessing for the *Sacerdotium*. The religious ceremonies were often interpreted as giving the kings a quasi-sacerdotal character, sometimes even miraculous healing powers. The kings were now thought of in Old Testament terms as the 'Lord's Anointed', set by God over Christian society, and this *Rex-Sacerdos* (King-Priest) conception linked up easily with the earlier Roman and Byzantine theory of Caesaro-papism. Some of the monarchs did not hesitate to extend their claims to supremacy over the clerical body itself, not excluding the Pope.

In 796 Charlemagne (768–814), the greatest of the Frankish kings and undisputed ruler of the west after his extensive conquests in Germany, Italy and Spain, sent a letter to Pope Leo III (795–816), in which he defined his own task as king as being 'to defend by armed strength the holy Church of Christ everywhere from the external onslaught of the pagans and the ravages of the infidels and to strengthen within it the knowledge of the Catholic Faith'. The letter assigns to the Pope the purely passive duty of praying for his people.

The revival of the Western Roman Empire on Christmas

24

Day, 800, when Leo III crowned Charlemagne in Rome as Emperor, restated the problem in its old terminology— *Sacerdotium* and *Imperium*. We are still by no means certain of the real meaning of the famous ceremony; the chief participants may not have been quite certain about it themselves. What we can say is that in the century after the coronation the idea grew up that the new dignity had been conferred for the protection of Latin Christendom and that this protective function was symbolized by its connection with Rome.

The new Western Empire was, unlike its older Byzantine cousin, specifically created as an authority for the ordering of the Christian Commonwealth. It depended, not on the absolutism ascribed to the monarch by the tradition of Roman law, but on the belief that it was the trustee for the government of Latin Christendom. The future was to show whether it was to be superior or subordinate to the Papacy in this mission.

The collapse of the Empire of Charlemagne's descendants did not put an end to the new tradition of Western Empire. In 962 the Saxon king of Germany, Otto I (936–973), was crowned Emperor in Rome after a victorious expedition to North Italy and so inaugurated a permanent association of the Christian Roman Empire with the German kingdom. Under Otto's successors, particularly Otto III (983–1002), the revived Empire stood forth as the self-conscious rival of Byzantium. Otto III, son of a Byzantine princess, aspired to renovate not only the ancient Roman Empire, of which the Eternal City was to be once again the effective capital, but the Papacy itself.

The practical alternative to imperial control for the Papacy at this stage was manipulation by local factions at Rome; so reforming circles within the Church might have felt that, Caesaro-papist or not, the Emperor was on the side of the angels. The appointment of worthy imperial nominees such as Sylvester II (999–1003), the greatest scholar and (according to some) the greatest magician of his age, was a blow for the cause of reform. Later still Henry III (1039–1056) carried on

25

the tradition of imperial action to promote reform within the Church and Papacy, and received testimonials for his work from such ardent reformers as St. Peter Damian (*d.* 1072) and Cardinal Humbert (*d.* 1061), both associates of Hildebrand, the future Gregory VII. Yet the deeper implication of the imperial reforming policy was that the Papacy was in the Western Emperor's gift.

So a tradition of imperial supremacy over both clerical and secular branches of Christian society was being built up. This is not to say that papalist rival theories were lacking. Ninth-century Pontiffs such as Nicholas I (858–868) and John VIII (872–882) claimed extensive rights of political supervision over Christendom, a term of which John VIII seems to have been, if not the coiner, at least one of the first users. One of Nicholas's contemporaries accuses him of behaving as if he were 'Emperor of the whole world'. There was even a tendency to allege that the imperial power itself was derived from the Pope. The circumstances of Charlemagne's coronation lent colour to this, and a legend originating in the sixth century, and finally embodied in a forged document known as 'the Donation of Constantine' went further still, and declared that the fourth-century Emperor on his conversion had handed over the whole Western Empire to Pope Sylvester I. Gregory VII (1073–1085) seems to have made use of this legend (accepted by his time as a historical fact) in claiming feudal jurisdiction over western countries like Spain.

In one important respect the course of practical events was in clear discrepancy with both papal and imperial dreams of a unified Christian Commonwealth. Everywhere in western Europe after the fall of the Carolingians the political and economic barometers were set towards a fragmentation of society. The comparative collapse of trade and commerce made Europe at basis a collection of small, self-sufficient agricultural units. The latest series of barbarian invasions by Viking and Magyar in the ninth and tenth centuries had strengthened the existing tendency to look for protection to local strong men rather than to the central government of the titular monarchs. The personal connection between lord and vassal now crystallized into definite formulas of personal allegiance and loyalty, expressed in ceremonies of homage and fealty almost as elaborate as the monarchical coronation rituals.

The king's authority was not indeed questioned but it receded to a further remove. The kings themselves, imbibing the contemporary atmosphere, came to think of themselves not as monarchs of Roman or Byzantine type but as lords at the head of a pyramid of personal loyalties. In the great French eleventh-century epic poem, *The Song of Roland*, the king's chief vassals are 'the peers of France' and Charlemagne in the poem is little more than the chief among them. France in the tenth and eleventh centuries offers the extreme example of the decomposition of royal power in favour of the great vassal dukes and counts, though the Capetian dynasty of kings (from 987) clung to the prestige and aura of the old monarchical tradition and kept it alive against better days.

Elsewhere the centrifugal process did not go so far; England escaped it by the accident of the Norman Conquest while in Germany the personal abilities of the monarchs down to the thirteenth century did something to retard it. But broadly speaking the tendency everywhere is for the small local unit to become the focal point of society. The only real agency of solidarity left at this stage was the sense that all belonged to the *respublica Christiana*, the Christian Commonwealth. The role of the Church in the formation of the medieval attitude to political life was to be decisive.

$$\text{┼┼┼┼┼┼┼┼┼┼┼┼┼┼┼┼┼┼┼┼┼┼┼┼┼┼┼┼┼┼┼┼┼┼┼┼┼}$$

CHAPTER III

THE PROBLEM OF AUTHORITY WITHIN THE CHRISTIAN COMMONWEALTH

WHAT was the principle of government behind this *respublica Christiana* and how could its nature be assessed? The differing viewpoints on this question composed the first great polemical controversy in European thought on the nature, scope and limits of government.

The common description of the struggle as a conflict between Church and State is misleading; the Church and State problem in its modern sense of a tension between two separate societies with different aims did not exist in the eleventh century. The conflict was rather one between different branches of one and the same society. To describe the protagonists in the struggle as the Empire and the Papacy is an over-simplification, for other forces were involved, even if they less often took the centre of the stage. Even the current academic preference for *Sacerdotium* and *Regnum* as the two terms in this historical antithesis has its drawbacks; not every cleric was an unflinching supporter of the rights of the *Sacerdotium*, while some of the staunchest adherents of the Papacy were often secular monarchs and lords or *bourgeois* townsfolk. The truth is that here, as in most historical problems, no terminology can correspond perfectly to the shifting reality of the actual situations and events.

In the Empire the struggle described by modern historians as the Investiture Contest can be shown to be a three-cornered conflict between a secularized episcopate (anxious to preserve its customary prerogatives against papal centralization), the imperial power (which saw papal centralization as a menace to its own monarchical authority) and the Papacy (which saw centralization as the only way to a reformed and

28

purified Church). From another aspect the same conflict can be seen as a political struggle between a centralizing monarchy and its particularist opponents, such as the Saxons in Germany and the Lombard towns in Italy. In the polemical statements of the period we find reflections of all these aspects; but over and above them all is the sense, felt by all parties, that this is a dispute about the government of a unified Christian society.

Sacerdotium and *Regnum* alike, as good disciples of Gelasius, were prepared to allow the other a permanent part in such governing activity; each was ready to recognize to the other practical control over a certain demarcated sphere; and each, in the process of claiming elbow-room for its own task, often made root-and-branch criticism of the way in which its rival was performing its task. Finally each at various stages of the conflict claimed, or countenanced the claim for itself of supremacy over the other, with all the energy and bitterness of a family quarrel.

The personal duel between Gregory VII and Henry IV caught posterity's imagination. Yet their struggle was not the first or last act of the whole drama and their respective ideas and viewpoints were unique only in the intensity with which they were expressed. The Gregorian Reformation within the Church began before Gregory. The cry for the emancipation of members of the *Sacerdotium* from a corrupting lay control, whether exercised from the residence of king or lay patron or from the bed of the priest's wife or mistress, had long been a commonplace among the demands of clerical reformers; nor had Popes and bishops of preceding centuries been backward in claiming to be the mouthpieces of Christian law and morality. Gregory VII and his circle were however the first to attempt a bold practical application of the reforming ideals.

The time was indeed ripe. By the middle of the eleventh century the See of Peter was coming forward as the one ecclesiastical institution which had the capability of freeing the Church from the corruption to which secular control had led it. The Papacy had felt strong enough in 1059 to shake off

29

imperial interference by vesting control of papal elections in the College of Cardinals, originally leading ecclesiastics of the local church of Rome. The new German monarch, Henry IV (1056–1106), was still too young to vindicate imperial rights and the new model Papacy, with a deacon of genius, Hildebrand, as its Cromwell, proceeded to build up secular support for itself in anticipation of the imperial reaction which was bound to come sooner or later.

In southern Italy the Papacy came to terms with the Norman freebooters who were gradually taking over what was to become their kingdom of Naples and Sicily, and which they actually held from the Papacy from 1059 onwards as a papal fief. In the north of Italy the Popes tampered with the loyalty of technical subjects of the imperial dynasty by encouraging radical elements in the Lombard towns to revolt against the imperially appointed bishops. The biggest threat to the German monarchy came from the Papacy's encouragement of the frequent and stubborn rebellions of the Saxons against the Franconian Imperial house.

When open conflict finally came between Henry and Hildebrand, now Gregory VII (1073–1085), it arose as a result of the Gregorian attack on the practice of lay investiture of bishops and abbots. By the eleventh century the control by the lay patrons of offices high and low in the Church had become widespread. Humanly speaking the system was not unreasonable: most of the religious establishments of the time owed their existence and continuance to benefaction by a noble patron and his descendants and Germanic property conceptions saw nothing wrong in the notion that he who provided the funds for a religious benefice should thereby gain the right to appoint its incumbent. For the monarchy the bishops of the realm would be the most competent available administrative agents and royal control of their appointment would therefore be considered as essential. By the time of Gregory VII this control had taken symbolic form in a ceremony derived from current secular feudal practice. The monarch handed over to the new bishop the ring and crozier, visible signs of episcopal authority, and in return received from him an act of homage. It was this practice of investiture that the papalist reformers singled out as the biggest single cause of unworthy members and relaxed standards in the *Sacerdotium*.

The investiture problem was not peculiar to Germany and Italy. The practice was current in every part of western Europe. But given the close ideological connection which had developed between the papal and imperial dignities as respectively the twin branches of Latin Christian society, it was inevitable that it should be their mutual conflict which was fought out with most sound and fury.

The battle was punctuated by exchanges of depositions and excommunications. Henry riposted to Gregory's prohibition of lay investiture and its application in 1075 to the test case of the archbishopric of Milan by declaring Gregory deposed. This drew upon Henry a counter-deposition from Gregory, and the rebel Saxons were able to use this to such advantage that in 1077 Henry was forced to secure absolution from Gregory after his famous and humiliating journey to Canossa.

After a lull, which Henry used to inflict a crushing defeat on the Saxons, the conflict was resumed in 1080 with the usual exchange of discourtesies. This time Henry was in the stronger political position and Gregory was on the run, sometimes even in a literal sense, for the rest of his reign. In 1084 he was expelled from Rome itself and died in exile with his Norman allies in the south.

In such a hectic and dramatic pontificate Gregory took little care to preserve consistency in legal theory. From the standpoint of later canonistics his sentence in 1076 against Henry IV might seem to place the cart before the horse by making the pronouncement of Henry's excommunication follow instead of precede that of his deposition. A more carefully canonical theory might have made clear that Henry's loss of his right to rule was a result of his expulsion from

31

Christian society as a consequence of his rebellion against its papal head; Gregory himself adopts this more logical sequence of ideas in his second condemnation of Henry in 1080. Yet it seems that for him the two concepts of religious excommunication and political deposition were not very distinctly separated; they were simultaneous expressions of the fact that Henry had put himself outside the pale of a rightly ordered Christian society.

The same conflation of what the modern would prefer to distinguish as the religious and political spheres respectively appears in the set of propositions known as the *Dictatus Papae*. For our present purpose it is irrelevant whether this document was actually drawn up by Gregory in person or whether it formed the headings of an otherwise lost canonical collection. Even if the *Dictatus* is not by Gregory himself it clearly comes from his *milieu* and it is significant that one of its main features is an apparently indiscriminate juxtaposition of maxims relating to ecclesiastical and secular affairs. 'That he (the Pope) may depose Emperors' (proposition 12) is followed immediately by 'That he may transfer bishops, if necessary, from one see to another' (proposition 13); this abrupt transition is quite in keeping with Gregory's characteristic conflation of two fields of Christian authority.

For a clear personal expression of Gregory's case we must turn to his letters to Bishop Hermann of Metz (1076 and 1081). To this wavering German bishop Gregory addresses his most famous *pièces justificatives*. The authorities cited in both letters are themselves largely papal, his namesake Gregory the Great being the most frequently quoted. It was no accident that Gregory VII and his circle should be the agency which gave the deciding impetus to the construction of a universally applicable canon law based in large measure on the past pronouncements of the Roman See. St. Augustine, so often alleged to have been the formative influence on Gregory VII, is in fact only quoted once in the letters to Hermann; this scantiness of reference is a fair indication of Gregory's lack of much first-class knowledge of the *corpus* of Augustine's writings. He does, however, seem to derive from a fundamental Augustinian antithesis between the city of the world and the city of God.

The royal *Regnum* and *Sacerdotium* are sharply contrasted in such phrases as: 'Human pride invented the one (i.e. the secular kingship), Divine goodness instituted the other. The one unceasingly hankers after vainglory, the other always aspires to heavenly life' (from the first letter). In the second letter Gregory pursues the same argument even more violently: 'Who does not know that kings and princes are sprung from those who, unmindful of God, urged on in fact by the devil, the prince of the world, and by pride, plunder, treachery, murders and by almost every crime, have striven with blind cupidity and intolerable presumption to dominate over their equals, that is to say, over men?'

This has sometimes been regarded as tantamount to an assertion of the diabolical origin of secular power; if this were indeed the case, it would have to be admitted that, even allowing for the exceptionally irritating circumstances under which he wrote, Gregory's language was well outside the main stream of Christian thought on politics. But it seems more likely that Gregory did not intend such extreme implications to be drawn from his words. He was expressing once again the Augustinian theory that God allowed sometimes the exercise of authority by unjust rulers as a punishment for human sin.

The main theme of these letters of Gregory is the superiority of the *Sacerdotium* to its secular rival. From this pre-eminence, which both sides acknowledged, Gregory deduced a more controversial claim—the right of the *Sacerdotium* and particularly the Papacy to excommunicate a delinquent monarch and absolve his subjects from their oaths of fealty to him. Gregory gave his claim its most forceful enunciation in the words of his second sentence of deposition of Henry IV in 1080 when he calls on the heavenly witnesses SS. Peter and Paul to witness the power of the earthly Papacy to deprive

33

rulers of their dignities and bestow them upon others. This forthright assertion crystallizes the whole objective of Gregory's stormy pontificate. He claims for the Papacy the ultimate direction of an indivisible Christian society.

It cannot be said that Henry's official counter-claims have the same consistency as the Gregorian platform. At the start of the long conflict he takes his stand on familiar Caesaro-papist lines. In his famous letter from Utrecht in 1076, summoning Gregory to abandon his usurped papal dignity, he asserts the Divine right of imperial power and denies that the Papacy has any authority to control its exercise. Later in the same year, in a letter calling the bishops of Germany to a Diet at Worms, Henry's arguments become strangely dualist, advocating a complete separation between the spheres of priesthood and kingship. The letter introduces to the controversy the celebrated theory of the two swords, based on the type of allegorical argument which was so dear to the medieval mind. The enigmatic remark of Christ, as reported in St. Luke's Gospel, confirming the possession of two swords by the Apostles, was taken by Henry's letter to be an allegorical portrayal of the spiritual and temporal powers. From the fact that the swords in question were two in number, the letter argues, *Regnum* and *Sacerdotium* should not be in the same hands. In espousing this strict dualism Henry was not only checking the temporal pretensions of the Papacy but also tacitly abandoning the cherished Imperial *Rex-Sacerdos* theory itself. There is some plausibility in a recent suggestion that Henry's draughtsman for this letter was Gottschalk of Aachen, an original if eccentric theologian, and that it is to him that this novel imperial dualism is to be attributed. Later still at the Synod of Brixen in 1080, which declared Gregory deposed for the second time, Henry returned to the more usual Caesaro-papism of his predecessors.

The struggle for the supreme leadership of Christian society also had implications for what may be described as the internal constitutional development of both *Sacerdotium* and

Regnum. Neither Pope nor King lived in a vacuum. Beneath each of them extended a varied hierarchy of subordinate authorities, every grade of which enjoyed or claimed its own particular prerogatives, rights and duties *vis-à-vis* its monarch. The Pope had his territorial episcopate and, nearer home, his College of Cardinals. The King had his feudal vassals, secular and ecclesiastical, and his non-feudal subjects, who owed allegiance to him, not as overlord but as national or tribal monarch. Elements in both these hierarchies seized the opportunity of the clash between their respective monarchs to emphasize and enforce their own rights. The result is that, while from one angle the conflict may be treated as a civil war between the two main branches of Christian society, from another it may be considered as a series of civil wars within each of these two branches.

Let us consider the situation within the sacerdotal hierarchy first. The Gregorian age marks the first great Papal effort to acquire effective centralized control of the administrative machinery of the Church where such machinery existed and to create it where it did not. In order to attain this objective the Papacy from Leo IX onwards (perhaps even before) set itself to codify in a uniform legal system the voluminous and sometimes inconsistent canonical legislation of the various local divisions of the Church. The practice of visitation in local Church provinces by papal legates, direct emissaries from the Pope, aimed at inspecting and controlling the government of the local bishops and clergy and correcting abuses.

The reaction of the episcopate to this closer proximity of papal power was mixed. Some bishops, identifying Rome with the reforming cause, welcomed it; others regarded the new tendency as an unwarranted diminishing of their own canonical rights. They would have allowed the Pope an undefined doctrinal supremacy but wished to curtail his supervision of the administration of their own dioceses. It is not surprising that this group, particularly in Germany, should support the

35

Regnum as an ally against the dictatorial tendencies of the head of the *Sacerdotium*. Henry IV, some of whose closest advisers were bishops, knew how to appeal to this anti-papal mentality in the territorial bishops; his letter from Utrecht in 1076 even accuses Gregory of treading down the episcopate 'as if they were servants with no knowledge of what their master may do'. At the Synod of Brixen in 1080 the bishops were in the forefront of the battle against Gregory and his policies.

The natural reaction of those bishops who considered the Emperor as less of a menace to their cherished autonomy than the Pope would be to subscribe to the *Rex-Sacerdos* theory, which gave the secular monarch supreme power over both branches of Christian society and hence over both hierarchies. Thus Archbishop Wenrich of Trier argued for the direct divine origin of royal authority and the consequent necessity of absolute submission to its commands by all, including the *Sacerdotium* itself.

This may seem a strange stand for a bishop to take but it is not so strange if one remembers that Wenrich, like many of his colleagues, was anxious to use any stick, even a secular one, provided it could beat the Pope. The strange Anglo-Norman writer often known as the Anonymous of York (though he may in fact have come from Rouen) went still further in depreciation of the Papacy by casting in doubt the legitimacy even of its spiritual supremacy. For the Anonymous the *Regnum* was clearly superior to the *Sacerdotium* because it represented Christ's Divine Nature as Ruler of the Universe, while the *Sacerdotium* typified His Human Nature as expressed in His priestly mediation between God and Man. As the Lord's Anointed the King has the right to govern the Church. In some ways the Anonymous may be seen in the line of the traditional *Rex-Sacerdos* theory, with its *mystique* of the semi-magical powers conferred on the monarch at the ceremony of his anointing; but in his forthright assault on papal government of the *Sacerdotium* the intrepid Anglo-Norman unknown seems to go far beyond any other writer of his time.

36

Not only from the bishops did resentment arise against the rapid advance of practical papal authority over the *Sacerdotium*. There were murmurings even among the Pope's own *corps d'élite*, the College of Cardinals. In 1084 thirteen of them deserted him and one, Benno of St. Martin, wrote an *apologia* for their action, in which he complained that Gregory had not given the Sacred College their due share of participation in conducting the affairs of the Church. Benno is voicing the protest of a monarch's group of advisers against what they consider to be the monarch's arbitrary infringement of their rights.

The current of resistance against abuse of monarchical power was not confined to the *Sacerdotium*. The *Regnum* too had its rebels with their grievances. A strong monarch who attempted to exert a more effective control of his territories was bound to fall out with tenacious local particularisms. Just as the Pope met with resistance from a section of his bishops, so the King met with resistance from his feudal and provincial magnates or from the new communities of the revived towns, with their ambition towards autonomy. Both these secular elements were only too ready to call in the head of the *Sacerdotium* to help them abase the power of the monarch, just as bishops and cardinals were ready for the same purpose to appeal to the head of the *Regnum*. In either case distance lent enchantment to the less immediately dangerous master. Thus it was that Henry IV's most determined opponents and Gregory VII's most loyal supporters were to be found among the Saxon provincial nobility of northern Germany and the Lombard urban *bourgeoisie* of northern Italy.

A specimen polemist of the anti-royal opposition may be found in Manegold of Lautenbach, a Saxon monk who wrote a spirited defence of the right of his compatriots to rebel against Henry IV. Manegold, arguing against Wenrich of Trier's statement that in no circumstances could a subject's oath of fealty to his monarch be broken, audaciously compared the kingship with the office of a swineherd.

37

The King, says Manegold, is appointed by his people for the express purpose of providing good government, just as the swineherd is hired for the preservation of the beasts put in his charge. If the swineherd does his job badly he may reasonably be dismissed; why should the King be exempt from this principle? He should in fact be dealt with much more severely than the delinquent swineherd, as the nature of men is higher than that of pigs and the penalty for mishandling them should therefore be correspondingly greater. Manegold's categorical assertion of the derivation of kingship from the community and the power of the community to terminate its grant of royal authority for a good reason bears resemblances to the Social Contract political theory of more modern times. But Manegold probably intended it as a forceful enunciation of the traditional rights which his Germanic community was resolved not to forego. As a cleric Manegold makes much of Henry's ecclesiastical and even moral offences and has no doubt that Gregory is within his rights in excommunicating him and depriving him of the kingdom. But it is the voice of outraged Saxon particularism which is predominant.

During the Gregorian period the original issue of investitures had been pushed into the background in favour of disputes about the larger claims to administrative direction of the Christian Commonwealth which both Pope and Emperor had been provoked into making. In the later period of struggle between Gregory's successors and Henry V (1106–1125) the larger conflict narrowed down once more to the specific investiture question. It was natural that both King and Pope should regard the conferring of the ring and staff as a touch-stone of their rival claims to authority in Christian society.

As the *impasse* created by these claims became clearer, there were attempts on both sides to find a way out. Guy of Ferrara, a supporter of Henry IV, had distinguished between a bishop's spiritual powers and his temporal goods and rights (the so-called *regalia*), the latter being legitimately subject to

38

royal control, as their very name might imply. The distinction was perhaps originally borrowed from defenders of the simon-, iacal buying of Church offices from the lay power but it was later taken up as a basis for a settlement by moderate papalists such as Ivo of Chartres, whose canonistic reputation did much to popularize the theory. In 1111 Pope Paschal II (1099–1118) used such a distinction as the basis of his proposed formula for settling the whole dispute by a complete renunciation of temporalities by the *Sacerdotium*.

The scheme proved unworkable as it would have damaged too many vested interests in both secular and ecclesiastical society. But Paschal's proposal, out of step with the realities of his time as it was, marks the first influential move towards a permanent division of the two branches of a western European society which had been regarded as a unity at least since the time of Charlemagne. Contemporary opinion was well aware of the radical character of the new proposal, which pleased neither side. Intransigent Gregorians like Godfrey of Vendôme even considered ceasing to recognize Paschal as Pontiff because of his heresy. Thus Paschal's political defeatism led to threats of constitutional rebellion within the *Sacerdotium* just as had Gregory's attempt at political domination.

In the event the investiture quarrel was ended by a compromise at Worms in 1122. This provided that in Germany the Emperor should confer the episcopal *regalia* only and should do so by the purely temporal symbol of the sceptre before consecration. He still retained the important right of appointment. In the Italian and Burgundian parts of the imperial realm, however, he lost this right to the local canonical authorities, who regained freedom of election. In these territories the investiture of *regalia* could follow consecration. The issue had been settled in England by a compromise on the same lines (though its details are still obscure) in 1107. In France the papal position had been accepted at a still earlier stage; the Capetian monarchy thus inaugurated its policy of posing, by contrast with the German sovereigns, as the good boy in the papal nursery.

Summing up the results for political development of the half-century of conflict between *Sacerdotium* and *Regnum*, we may say at once that it had brought into strong relief the claim in both secular and ecclesiastical hierarchies for the right of the community concerned to admonish and even depose its ruler if he failed in his obligations to his subjects. In both cases also the ruler countered this claim by appeal to what he declared to be his divinely given authority. This antithesis was to provide ever-increasing problems for medieval thought and behaviour, though more refined intellectual and legal instruments were necessary before these problems could find their full expression.

The other important result was due not so much to the principles at stake in the conflict itself as to the manner of its settlement. At Worms both *Regnum* and *Sacerdotium* had accepted the idea that there could be a valid distinction between the temporal and spiritual prerogatives of the episcopal office. This first separation between ecclesiastical and secular was in due course to be applied to other social functions beside that of bishop; in the very long run it was even to be applied to the whole of the social fabric of Christendom. The final dissolution of the unified religio-political Christian Common-wealth was still far from envisaged at the period of the Worms agreement; there was still no place for two separate and self-sufficient entities called Church and State. But it can reasonably be contended that the unsuspected medieval origins of their modern separation are to be sought in the age of the Investiture Contest.

CHAPTER IV

TWELFTH-CENTURY DISCOVERIES

THE twelfth century has a strong claim to be considered as
the first period in which the creative originality of the new
mixed Latin and Germanic society of western Europe had the
chance to show itself. For the first time the western nations are
doing more than stumble awkwardly in the steps of Rome and
Byzantium. Everywhere there is an air of freshness and the
sensation of advance towards new horizons. The impression is
not illusory. The first soarings of Gothic architecture, new
departures in philosophy and religious experience, fresh forms
of literature and art—even such an inadequate catalogue gives
a pointer to the almost wanton fertility of the age.

It is now generally agreed that the background to this
twelfth-century renaissance of culture was a far-reaching
economic renaissance in the eleventh century, and even before.
A series of remarkable changes, unequalled before the scientific
and industrial revolutions of modern times, gradually shifted
the balance of economic strength from the eastern Mediterranean to western Europe—a feat which the Roman Empire
itself had not accomplished. Agriculture led the way by a
variety of improved techniques, particularly in methods of
food cultivation. The consequent increase in food production
led to an increase in population and this in turn led to the
utilization and colonization of unexploited land, as well as an
expansion into new lands, both in Europe and the Near East.
The first western colonialism advanced under the crusading
banners against Slavs in central Europe and against Moslems
and Byzantines in the western and eastern Mediterranean.

The general advance in agriculture led also to the loosening
of the rigid structure of feudal economy. There was now a
surplus both of produce and of labour, the old bonds of

41

serfdom began to change slowly into forms of monetary connection between landlord and peasant, and many of the latter class were emigrating to seek their fortunes in those parts of Europe which were being reclaimed from forest, marsh or sea. If, like the Unjust Steward of the Gospel, they were not able to dig and were ashamed to beg, they might prefer to set up as merchants in the reviving towns.

The growth of the towns is the most striking index of the new world which was emerging. The surplus of agricultural produce had resulted in free circulation of goods outside the old limits of village and local district. A real all-European market was now possible and the towns, stagnant since the fall of Rome, revived to fulfil their inevitable role as the entrepots and communication centres for the new trading network of western Christendom. Improvement in communications made a mobile economy of buying and selling again possible in the west. Money and precious metals again played their full part in the creation of a sophisticated high life and a rise in the standard of living all down the social scale was reflected in a corresponding rise in prices. The master of ceremonies in this whole process was the indispensable merchant, a shopkeeper, banker, pedlar rolled into one, still very peripatetic but already tending to use the towns as his bases. The new trading and commercial classes of the towns could not settle into the straitjacket of the feudal order, and the towns became a chief agent in its final disruption.

The great economic and social changes gave more leisure for learned and artistic activity for a section of the population at least. The privileged higher orders of the secular and ecclesiastical hierarchies had time and money to patronize cultural pursuits even where they did not actively follow them. Artists and builders could hardly have originated or perfected the wonderful output of Gothic architecture without the financial assistance provided by the monied upper classes. Those new oases of learning, the universities, admittedly issued from the perennial human craving for knowledge and discussion,

42

stimulated by the rediscovery of intellectual treasures of the past; but they could not have continued without the backing of kings, nobles and Popes, anxious to make use of the new type of learned clerk which only the discipline of the universities could provide.

This collaboration in art and learning of the two qualities of inventive originality and enlightened patronage points to an even deeper synthesis of disparate elements which was attempted by the age as a whole. The twelfth century was in all its aspects at once a period of highly individualist complexity and of growing centralization and co-ordination. The Angevins in England, the Capetians in France, the Hohenstauffen in Germany and Italy, all attempted in their various ways to make use of legal and local complexities in their realms to build thereon a strong central power. This *tour de force* in political activity was paralleled in political thinking by a more intensely felt belief that a society was a corporate organism, a body politic.

We can see this corporate view of political society in the thought of one of the most versatile humanists of the century, John of Salisbury (*c.* 1115–1178). John's *Policraticus*, written in the 1150s, is a description of what a ruler ought to be (a type of literary exercise which had a great vogue during the medieval period) and may be taken as a specimen of the political thought current in the academic university circles in which John was so much at home. Perhaps the adjective academic is a little inaccurate when applied to such circles, for from them came most of the trained administrators of the time in both *Regnum* and *Sacerdotium*. John's work forms an invaluable revelation of how this class of politically able and intellectually self-conscious clerks analysed the objectives and methods of their political activity. The clerks were indeed the only people in this age who could have analysed anything at all in systematic terms. It is significant, though no doubt improper, that members of this same clerical class at this same time were launching western literature on its long exploration of the emotional complexities of human love.

43

John makes use of all the classical learning available to his time; his book is a storehouse of quotations and echoes from classical authors, as well as from the Scriptures. Cicero is particularly in evidence and it may be assumed that it was from him that John took the inspiration to define his *respublica*. But John's commonwealth, unlike Cicero's, is under a monarch, and an absolute one at that, though John emphasizes that the good king should consider himself bound to observe the law. There is no explicit constitutional check on the king if he abuses his power, but John admits a 'right of resistance' and his classical training even leads him to state that an unjust king may be forcibly removed by tyrannicide.

On the whole, however, John is clear that the authority of the monarch must not be lightly challenged. After all, the prince is the representative of the entire community (he 'bears the person of the whole body (*universitas*) of his subjects'). He is to the body politic what the head is to the physical body of an individual man. The other components of the body politic may also be grouped according to physical counterparts and John pursues his metaphor with a thoroughness sometimes bordering on indelicacy.

The organic view of political society which was coming to the fore in John's lifetime had found more massive expression in the revival of Roman law. The Roman legal tradition had never of course been entirely forgotten by western Europe but its definitive codification at Byzantium by Justinian in his famous sixth-century collections had never been operative in the west except to a limited degree in Italy. The eleventh century saw a great effort to regain knowledge of Roman law in its classical form; developing western society needed a more elaborate legal pattern than could be provided by the old barbarian codes. So the juristic *corpus* of Justinian was dissected in its three main divisions as arranged by the Emperor's legal experts. These were the *Institutes* (a compendium), the *Digest* (a large but selective collection of previous laws) and the *Novellae* (new imperial laws).

44

By the twelfth century these were known in Italian legal centres in their entirety and the University of Bologna had established itself as the authoritative seat of study and interpretation of the civil law (*Jus Civile*), as Roman law was called (to distinguish it from the canon law of the Roman Church) during the Middle Ages. Most of the leading commentators on civil law either studied or taught at Bologna at some stage at least of their career. These commentators are usually known as the glossators, because they conceived their task to be one of writing explanations or glosses on the actual wording of the classical texts. Their work reached its consummation in the *Great Gloss* of Accursius (*c.* 1225), one of the most famous of the Bologna masters of legal science.

One of the leading concepts which the glossators were interested to find in Roman jurisprudence was that of the universal and timeless natural law. As we have seen, this was no novelty to medieval Christian thought, but the glossators were able to bring to western Christendom direct knowledge of the various meanings given to natural law by the authorities preserved in Justinian's Code. Confronted with the differences of approach among the authors quoted in the *Digest*, the glossators tended to vacillate between the view associated with Ulpian (third century A.D.), who held that natural law was an instinctive quality which men shared with other animals, and the rival view which regarded it as something essentially rational and therefore peculiarly human. All agreed that natural law formed the yardstick by which civil and other subordinate legal enactments might be judged and, if necessary, condemned and corrected. The principle of adjustment of defective laws by the use of right reason or equity passed from Roman law into the fabric of subsequent European legal systems. The glossators however differed among themselves on the question whether private reasoning or some recognized authority should be the arbiter in deciding where equity lay in a given case.

The Roman civil law itself was of course for these 'Civilian'

45

glossators the highest and standard form of human law. In commenting on it their first instinct was to interpret it in a literalistic fashion. But how would such an interpretation square with the changed realities of twelfth-century Europe? How could a body of law originating from a unitary centralized Empire be applied to a Europe still dominated by a veneration for its network of separate rights and customs?

Some glossators reacted to these problems by falling back into rigidity and pursuing a rather futile *de iure* argument in favour of supreme imperial authority over other kingdoms. But even in the palmiest days of the Hohenstauffen dynasty there was no chance of an imperial reunification of the west and most of the glossators were content to assert for the *Imperium* a merely nominal overlordship. At the same time their respect for the political framework expressed in the law was so great that they performed the *tour de force* of using the old classical vocabulary for discussion of contemporary political issues.

The chief of such issues was the growing power of the central monarchical principle in both *Sacerdotium* and *Regnum*. The study of Roman law provided a new instrument for the theoretical discussion of this power and its limits, if any. The famous statement of Ulpian (incorporated in Justinian's *Digest* as the so-called '*Lex Regia*') speaks of the monarch as being the agent of enforcement of law in these words: 'What pleases the prince has the force of law, because by the *lex regia*, which was made concerning his authority, the people confers to him and upon him all its own authority and power.' This clearly states that the Emperor's power derives from the Roman people; the doctrine underlying this quotation may fairly be described as one of popular sovereignty.

But when the glossators dealt with the passage, they found themselves faced with a question which had not occurred to Ulpian or Justinian: by submitting itself to the monarch, had the people renounced all right to political authority, or did it retain a final reserve of authority which it could exercise if it thought fit? More than an academic problem of textual interpretation was at stake here; what was at issue in contemporary terms was the right of the community to have a share in framing the law, either by direct legislation or through the claims of custom. It was a problem which we have seen confronting both *Sacerdotium* and *Regnum* during their mutual contest, though in that contest the terminology used to express the problem was an explicitly Christian one. Now for the first time the Civilians, dealing with the same basic problem, use terminology and a set of ideas which need not be specifically Christian.

The Civilians themselves gave varying answers to the problem. Some held that the people had always retained a residue of authority, others that it had irrevocably parted with all its authority to the Emperor. Irnerius, the first great name of the Bologna school (twelfth century), believed that the Emperor should consult with the Senate in making laws; in contemporary terms this was a restatement of the Germanic conviction that the making or interpretation of laws needed the co-operation of the community through its chief men.

This example of the interpretation of Roman and Germanic ideas is a useful reminder of the folly of regarding Roman law as embarking from the outset on a campaign against the particularist systems of feudal law. It is true that its emphasis on a strong central monarchy backed up the attempts of monarchs like Henry II of England (1154–1189) or Emperor Frederick I (1152–1190) to reclaim royal prerogatives which had been pushed into the background. But on the whole the Civilian lawyers tried to find a *modus vivendi* with feudal conceptions, just as the kings themselves used feudal custom to increase their own effective authority over their territorial nobility. So the loose fabric of feudal and customary law lived side by side with Roman law and achieved a greater precision and more logical presentation as a result of this contact. By an irony which was perhaps inevitable, feudal customs reach their clearest codification at the moment when feudal particularism itself is on the decline.

What effect did the ideas and methods of Roman law have on the other branch of Christian society, the *Sacerdotium*? Here too the twelfth century saw an accentuation of the process of centralization round a monarchical authority. Throughout the period after the Concordat of Worms, papal control over the different provinces of the Church became steadily more effective. Improvement in communications and travel enabled the Papacy to exercise closer supervision by means of legates and other officials in all local divisions of the Church, while a more conscientious episcopate gave greater co-operation to the See of Rome.

The Papacy was also able to utilize the impressively numerous new forms of Christian thought and action which are so noticeable in twelfth-century history. The papal leadership of the crusading movement against the Moslems, the papal patronage of reforming monastic movements like the Cistercians, the papal backing for the new establishments of study and teaching at the universities and finally the papal support for those excitingly novel men of God, the uncloistered orders of friars: all these are differing facets of a consistent bid by the Papacy to strengthen its age-long claim to act as the universal authority at the head of Christian society. It was understandable that this authority should seek to cement its control by sponsoring the formation of a comprehensive body of law, uniformly applicable throughout Christendom and superseding the local canonical collections of previous ages. This need had already been felt in the twelfth century but the legal compilations produced by the Gregorian reform suffered from a lack of a precise legal terminology and they were therefore bound to be superseded as the administrative system of the Church followed the general twelfth-century pattern in becoming both more complex and more subject to centralized control.

The revival of Roman civil law and the study of its methods suggested an obvious model for the construction of a papally orientated ecclesiastical legal code. But there remained the problem of varying, often contradictory authorities and precedents. Here a solution was provided by the contemporary dialectical techniques followed at the rising universities. The pattern of university education in the twelfth century and the whole subsequent medieval period was one of commentary on recognized authorities combined with debates in various forms on problems raised by the study of the authorities. The young University of Paris was to be for theology and philosophy what Bologna was for legal studies. Here the famous Peter Abelard (1079–1142) set his mind on other objectives besides the seduction of his beautiful bluestocking, Heloïse. In his *Sic et Non* he made a collection of conflicting sayings by patristic authorities on theological and philosophical questions and placed them side by side without suggesting a resolution of their differences. Abelard in fact believed that many disagreements were merely verbal and could be explained by a careful consideration of the exact sense in which the same words were used by different authorities. The same method was pursued later in the century in the same field by Peter Lombard (*d.* 1160) in his *Sentences*, which became the classic medieval theological textbook. Lombard however did attempt to resolve his material into a synthesis.

What Abelard and Lombard did for theology, the *Concordantia discordantium Canonum* (The Reconciliation of differing Canons), or, as it was more popularly called, the *Decretum*, did for canon law. It has usually been supposed that this work, which must have appeared round about 1140, was compiled by Gratian, a cleric of Bologna, at that centre of legal studies. But recent scholarly suggestions would have it that Gratian, like Homer, was not one but many, that the individual of that name was only one of a succession of collaborators and revisers and that the work may even have been compiled at Rome under the direct aegis of the Papacy.

Whatever the truth about these questions of authorship, the fact remains that within a generation the *Decretum* had become the standard textbook of canon law, memorized and

49

commented upon by its specialized interpreters, the decretists, all over the Catholic world, and forming the basis for a uniform legal code applicable everywhere. But canon law did not stand still after Gratian. The Popes were continually issuing new enactments in conformity with the needs of the times. These in turn were assembled and classified in the so-called decretal collections of the thirteenth and fourteenth centuries and commented upon by the decretalists just as Gratian's had been by the decretists. Both schools of commentators are referred to by modern historians under the collective designation of canonists. The most famous of canonist commentaries, the *Glossa Ordinaria*, was compiled in the early thirteenth century by Joannes Teutonicus (*d.* 1246) about the same time as the work on civil law of Accursius.

It is understandable that canon law, which took its method and terminology from civil law, should also incorporate some of its ideas. Thus the canonists universally depict the universe as ruled by a natural law of reason, though some of them follow Gratian in identifying natural law with the Divine law contained in Scripture. All of them tend to reject Ulpian's description of natural law as a matter of animal instinct; Rufinus, one of the leading decretists of the twelfth century, takes pride in indicating the canonistic rejection of Ulpian's view which he somewhat unfairly fathers on the Civilian lawyers in general by describing it as the *legistica traditio*.

Again, like civil law, canon law assumed the original personal equality of all men, but was prepared to allow institutions like slavery and property as inevitable results of a fallen society. The coercive authority of both *Sacerdotium* and *Regnum* is necessary for man's imperfect state; but under what conditions might these authorities be exercised? The decretists gave some interesting and varied answers to these questions. . . .

Canonist observations relevant to the development of political thought may be summarized for our purposes in two categories. The first of these is the relationship of the Pope to his own hierarchy, the *Sacerdotium,* and to the body of

Christian faithful in general; the second is his relationship to the other hierarchy of the Christian Commonwealth, the lay authority of the *Regnum*.

Following Gratian and the general line of tradition, the decretists saw the Papacy as the normal holder of the powers of binding and loosing committed by Christ to the Church in the person of St. Peter. But they could not help being aware that this normal process of government might on occasion break down or be severely handicapped. The recurrent nightmare was the possibility of an heretical Pope. The exact nature of papal doctrinal authority was still undefined by any dogmatic pronouncement and was to remain so until the Vatican Council of 1870. So a wide field of speculation was open to the decretists, who certainly availed themselves of it to the full.

A common method of meeting the difficulty was to argue that the promises made to Peter were made to the Roman Church not in any limited local sense but as symbolizing the whole body of faithful Christians. Huguccio of Pisa (*d.* 1210), probably the greatest of all the decretists, comments dryly in his *Summa* (unhappily still unprinted): 'Wherever honest faithful people are, there is the Roman Church; otherwise you will not find a Roman Church in which there are not many stains and many wrinkles.' This was the only Roman Church which was infallibly preserved from error; it was not necessary that all, or even the majority, should remain orthodox. As long as one individual remained faithful to the truth, Christ's promise would be preserved. The decretists did not consider it inevitable that that individual must be the Pope.

In normal times, moreover, the Pope's authority was by no means unlimited. Here we arrive at a significant difference between the problem confronting the canonists and that confronting the civilians. It was easy enough for the civilians to argue: 'What pleases the prince has the force of law', even if they recognized the rights of secular custom. The canonists could not use quite such strong language about the Pope, for besides the claims of legitimate local custom (which the

51

canonists recognized) the whole body of dogma laid down by the Scriptures and general councils of the Church could not be changed or modified by the Papacy. Most of the decretists after Gratian went further and argued that general councils were superior to the Pope in defining articles of faith, because they embodied the 'universal consent' of the whole Church, though they left this concept of consent rather vaguely defined. They assumed as axiomatic, however, that a Council needed the presence of the Pope to be a valid Council. So in practice their contention was that the Pope legislating for the Church with the assistance of a Council possessed greater authority than when legislating alone. The conception is reminiscent of the Germanic and feudal idea in secular politics that the king adds greater solemnity to his decisions by associating with them the great men of the kingdom.

Another more oligarchical variant of this theme is to be found in the *Glossa Palatina*'s opinion that the Pope cannot enact laws for the whole Church without the agreement of his Cardinals. The text is an indication of the increased importance of the Sacred College since the days of Benno's complaints against Gregory VII; the Consistory of Cardinals was now the normal assembly used as the vehicle for the proclamation of solemn papal decisions. The feudal secular parallel would be the small permanent body of officials in constant attendance on the king. And just as the king was thought of as being committed to preserve the customs of his kingdom, so the Pope was regarded as being committed to preserve the *status ecclesiae* (i.e. the traditional condition of the Church). The problem of the lawfulness of removing him if he did not do so was argued at some length by the decretists. Gratian himself had denied the possibility of the Pope being brought to judgement, except in his commentary on an enigmatic text attributed by him to St. Boniface (680–755), but actually deriving from Cardinal Humbert. Huguccio held that not only heresy but other crimes against the Church might be punishable by deposition 'to avoid danger and general confusion for the

Church'. However his offence must be public before proceedings ought to be taken. The *Glossa Ordinaria* seems to believe that in case of heresy the Pope may be subject to judgement by a general council, and Alanus, the famous English canonist of the early thirteenth century, puts this point of view quite unambiguously. The decretists did not trouble themselves much to explore the theoretical implications of these statements of legal possibility; they were not after all professional theologians or political philosophers. Yet their opinions certainly influenced both theology and political thought later on.

The second main problem, the relationship of *Sacerdotium* and *Regnum*, was of universal practical interest. Papal intervention in secular politics took place in a wide range of cases, of which the conflict with the Hohenstauffen dynasty was the outstanding example. The Papal-imperial imbroglio was largely centred on Italian questions and it was therefore with regard to the Empire that the Papacy felt the secular shoe pinch most. The Papacy always thought of itself as standing in a special relationship to the Empire because it had recreated the imperial institution in the west by elevating Charlemagne and by the Pope's traditional and exclusive right to carry out the imperial coronation at Rome.

In 1157 the legates of Adrian IV (1154–1159) to the Diet of Besançon were almost lynched by Frederick I's courtiers when they read the Pope's letter in which he spoke of having 'conferred *beneficia*' on Frederick. *Conferre beneficia* was an ambiguous phrase capable of meaning either 'to confer favours' or the more technically feudal 'to confer fiefs'. Adrian seems to have had the former sense in mind; after all he had given Frederick the imperial *regalia* in 1155. But Frederick and his German followers, more accustomed to the strictly feudal meaning, had jumped to the conclusion that Adrian was literally claiming to be Frederick's temporal overlord.

Later we find Innocent III (1198–1216) arguing in a famous decretal, *Venerabilem fratrem* (1202) that the Papacy has the right to confirm elections to the imperial office on the ground that the Papacy had transferred the Empire from the Greeks (i.e. the Byzantines) to the Germans in the days of Charlemagne. But this claim to supervision of the election to the Empire does not provide conclusive proof that there was any general papal claim to direct supremacy over the secular authority as such.

Nor is such proof provided by the feudal overlordship exercised over certain kingdoms by the Papacy. As far back as the eleventh century the practice had grown up whereby a kingdom might place itself under the protection of the Apostle Peter, in other words become a vassal of the Papacy. Hungary, Croatia, Aragon and the Norman kingdom of southern Italy provide examples of this, but the oath of vassalage for England taken to Innocent III by John (1199–1216) in 1213 will be more familiar to English readers. The Papacy certainly claimed a widespread and often resented authority over all these kingdoms; yet the basis of the claim in every case was not an abstract doctrine of *plenitudo potestatis* but a carefully defined feudal prerogative.

No Pope was more officially respectful of secular feudal rights than Innocent III and most of his massive interventions in the politics of his time were based theoretically on a deduction from his spiritual responsibilities. In the decretal *Novit Ille* (1204) Innocent claims the power to arbitrate between the warring kings of France and England on the ground that, though he claimed no judicial competence in their feudal disputes as such, his authority in cases where sin might be committed (*pro ratione peccati*) could not be denied. It is true that such a definition might be (and was) extended to cover almost any political activity, so in practice Innocent could enjoy an unlimited power of intervention. But the fact remains that he did not claim that power by virtue of any root-and-branch theory of universal temporal sovereignty.

Some twelfth-century writers have been interpreted as asserting that the secular government was completely derivative from the Papacy and was given a separate but subordinate authority for the down-to-earth task of preserving material order, the donkey-work of human society. In this context the often-used allegory of the two swords is quoted as evidence. We have already met this as a weapon used by Henry IV in his struggle with the Papacy. By the twelfth century it had been appropriated by the papalists, not without protest from Frederick Barbarossa. In the first quarter of the century Honorius of Augsburg (or Canterbury, as a recent theory would have it) used the Donation of Constantine as proof that the secular Christian power had handed over the material sword (*gladius materialis*), i.e. secular authority, to the *Sacerdotium* and had received it back to exercise under ecclesiastical supervision, while the *Sacerdotium* retained ultimate *de iure* possession of it. In the middle of the century John of Salisbury and St. Bernard of Clairvaux (1091–1153), both convinced upholders of the primacy of the Papacy as well as being personal friends of individual Popes, talk of the secular authority receiving the material sword (*gladius materialis*) from the *Sacerdotium*. John speaks of the prince as performing '. . . that part of the sacred offices which seems unworthy of priestly hands', while St. Bernard, in *De Consideratione*, a *vade-mecum* written specially for Pope Eugenius III (1145–1153), talks of both swords as belonging to the Church and says that 'the former (i.e. the spiritual) is to be drawn by the Church, the latter on behalf of the Church'. The exact meaning of these statements is doubtful, but at any rate they do seem to indicate a claim on behalf of the *Sacerdotium* to some kind of supervisory control. This does not necessarily mean that these writers have in mind a direct exercise of temporal power by the Papacy. The same may be said of the much-quoted remark of the theologian Hugh of St. Victor (1096–1141) that the *Sacerdotium* had the right to institute and judge the royal power; Hugh may be doing no more than make a reference to the Church's established right to anoint and crown a monarch and to supervise his observance of his oath to rule justly.

55

A recent student of the medieval canonists, A. M. Stickler, has argued that when Gratian used the term *gladius materialis*, he had in mind the Church's own coercive power over heretics and moral offenders, a power which the *Sacerdotium* itself could not exercise as it involved bloodshed and which was therefore delegated to secular authority. During the late twelfth and early thirteenth centuries, Stickler's theory goes on, a confusion of terminology among canonists led to the *Sacerdotium's* control of the *gladius materialis* being interpreted by some as a control of the secular authority as such. The work of Huguccio is seen as the turning-point in the conflation of the two meanings of *gladius materialis*. He made use of both senses in various parts of his work, though he distinguished carefully between them according to his context. If we accept Stickler's theory the statements of John of Salisbury and St. Bernard fall into a more moderate connotation, not far different from that of Gelasius himself.

As far as we can determine from our present imperfect knowledge of the decretists (most of whose works still remain unprinted), there seem to have been two schools of thought among them on the question of the Church's control over the secular power, which the twelfth-century canonists regarded as epitomized in the Emperor. The possession of the keys of St. Peter by the Papacy was interpreted by one school as implying a power at least of confirmation of the Emperor: the *Summa Lipsiensis* (1186) mentions an opinion that, as the Pope confers the material sword on the Emperor, he may also deprive the latter of it by deposition. The *Summa* itself prefers to support the Gregorian idea of the popular derivation of imperial authority and to confine the Papacy's role in deposing an Emperor to the initial step of excommunication, which would necessitate the withdrawal of allegiance from the Emperor by his subjects. Huguccio clearly separates the spheres of the two authorities in true Gelasian style but grants to the Pope the power to judge the Emperor even in secular affairs if the Emperor is at fault therein. He justifies this on the ground that the Emperor has no secular superior to whom those wronged by him can appeal. So the Pope, as the head of the superior hierarchy of the *Sacerdotium*, may be called on to provide justice. This very feudal tone of Huguccio's argument is also shown in his refusal to allow the Papacy the right to judge and depose secular authorities below the Emperor, for these have their own judicial superiors within their own hierarchy.

Innocent III, as befitted Huguccio's pupil, was aware of the differing spheres of spiritual and secular authority. He had no doubt of the superior nature of the *Sacerdotium's* dignity and talked of the spiritual as illuminating and ennobling the secular power, but he made no explicit claim to direct papal institution and control of the secular power in general, as distinct from the Empire in particular.

Looking back we can easily see the ambiguities in twelfth-century thought. Talk of the body politic could co-exist with a bewildering complexity of local privileges and jealously guarded customs. The rediscovery of the Roman tradition of centralized law came at a convenient moment in the struggle of the monarchical authority in each hierarchy of the Christian Commonwealth to maintain and strengthen its position. The Papacy pressed centralization hardest of all because the historical development of the century put at the Church's disposal a greater chance to achieve centralized control than any secular authority could yet hope for. But the secular monarchs were hot on the Papacy's trail. The Empire itself was to fall by the wayside because of its failure to create sufficient unity in its German and Italian dominions. But the Angevin dynasty and those late starters, the French Capetians, were making use of the local bodies of law and custom within their kingdoms to build an administrative system capable ultimately of challenging the Papacy's dominant position.

The new legal and political discoveries of the century did not work exclusively in the direction of strengthening central monarchical authority. The labours of commentators on both

57

civil and canon law raised indeed embarrassing problems for that authority. Civilian emphasis on the popular derivation of governmental authority transferred to a communal basis the primitive Germanic reliance on the right of resistance of individuals or groups to royal misrule. The decretists, concerned with the problem of the divinely-given papal authority, emphasized that the Pope was bound to take note of the *status Ecclesiae* in the exercise of his power. In both cases monarchical responsibility was coupled with increased monarchical power. For all the ambiguities and tensions which it left behind it, the twelfth century had succeeded in expressing in its own terms those fundamental problems of government and the governed which have become characteristic of the European political tradition.

CHAPTER V

THE BIRTH OF THE STATE

THE thirteenth century is regarded by many as the crowning age of medieval civilization and there is much to be said for this opinion. It was the age when Gothic architecture and sculpture achieved their classic formation and when there were new beginnings in painting and vernacular literature. In philosophy and theology the advance of the dialectical method of scholastic reasoning, together with the rediscovery of the works of Aristotle, gave a precise edge to the more ambiguous speculations of previous centuries. In economic life too the period was one of expansion due to the easier communications and the growth to maturity of the towns with their *bourgeois* merchant class, while concurrent steady increase in population found outlet in colonization of new lands in eastern and central Europe and the reconquest of Spain from the Moslems. Everywhere there was a tendency to greater complexity, in dress, in manners, in thought. In love or law, economics or ethics, men no longer found adequate the crude simplicities of the feudal world.

In political society also the old machinery of administration and government was no longer felt to be good enough. New methods had to be devised and new men had to be found to work them. The feudal council on which western monarchs had relied to provide support and sanction in interpreting customary law had already begun to feel the need for supplementary advice from various other classes of the community. These classes, *bourgeois* townsfolk, country gentlemen from the provinces of the realm, priests and lawyers were already called into consultation on occasion before the beginning of the thirteenth century. The feudal network of political and social relationships, even when manipulated by a clever king,

59

was no longer sufficient for all the monarch's purposes. He needed in addition some way of adjusting the traditional government processes to deal with his non-feudal subjects, who were constantly growing economically and politically more important. In particular he needed their collaboration in supplying him with the money he required. The thirteenth century saw a rising standard of living; the activities of war and peace were both now more costly. The king's private revenue and normal public dues were no longer sufficient to foot the bill; extra methods of taxation became necessary.

The king's problem was how to extract the extra money he needed as painlessly as possible from his subjects. It would obviously be impracticable to negotiate individually with everyone concerned; the king had neither the time nor the patience to do this. But he could achieve the same result by treating with the realm as a whole or with the different communities within it. This could only be done if those communities could be induced to appoint spokesmen to listen to the king's wishes and, more important, commit their communities to implement what he desired. In other words the western monarchs were moving towards a system of representation.

The ground for such a movement was already prepared by the corporate organizations which were being formed everywhere among the politically articulate sections of both *Regnum* and *Sacerdotium*. Trading guilds, associations, communal and civic councils and corporations, cathedral and monastic chapters all symbolized the proliferation of social units within medieval society and the need of each of these units to safeguard its autonomous existence. The *Regnum* itself began to be regarded as the corporation *par excellence* (if we exclude for the moment the Church) and the idea that the secular commonwealth was an organic body was given a more powerful legal development. The notion that the public authority of a realm had the right to demand contributions in case of emergency was justified by reference to such concepts as

60

utilitas regni or *necessitas regni,* untranslatable terms but obvious in their meaning. These terms go back beyond feudal or Germanic conceptions of royal prerogative to Roman law's theory of public utility and Aristotle's idea of the common good, while they seem to foreshadow dimly the modern idea of the State. In fact the word *status* itself began its transformation from meaning the general fabric of a community's customs and laws (written and unwritten) to meaning the supreme legislative authority within a social community. The word sovereignty itself was coined by French feudal lawyers of the later thirteenth century.

Here once more we must be on our guard against distinguishing too precisely between feudal and corporate ideas. The thirteenth century saw no absolute incompatibility between the king as feudal overlord and the king as public head of the whole political community. When a writer like Beaumanoir (*c.* 1250–1296) uses a word like sovereignty he certainly does not intend it to have the same significance as a modern thinker would attach to it; for him it is not the exclusive property of the public authority of the State. Beaumanoir was writing as a feudal lawyer, concerned to describe the local customs of his own district of France; his book is entitled simply *Les Coutumes des Beauvaisis.* So he can cheerfully say that 'each baron is sovereign in his own barony', a statement almost incomprehensible to us, with our clear-cut identification of sovereignty with the State. However, Beaumanoir, who had some acquaintance with Roman law, tried to account for the special position of the king by calling him 'the sovereign above all' and confining to him alone the power of making new laws or customs 'for the common profit'. Even here Beaumanoir is careful to limit the royal initiative in legislation by saying that it must be exercised with the advice of the great council of the realm and must not infringe religious or moral laws. Bracton (*d.* 1268), Beaumanoir's English counterpart, shows the same mixture of feudal and organic conceptions and the same formulation of a

61

locally peculiar common and customary law in terminology influenced by the *Corpus* of Justinian or at least by one of the medieval epitomes of it. The old conception of the king as bound by the law on the Germanic model is asserted by Bracton in a number of passages, though his general tendency is to deprecate any thought of external checks to enforce the fulfilment of the king's obligations. On the other hand he strongly emphasizes the institutional rather than the personal aspect of royalty when he denies that the king can ever lawfully alienate those essential judicial and administrative functions and qualities which make the Crown what it is.

The monarchy's desire to achieve a greater degree of assistance and co-operation from its non-feudal subjects did not immediately express itself in a full-fledged representative system. Henry II of England, Frederick Barbarossa and others had often consulted with their subjects in town and countryside by interviewing leading local personalities, obtaining information from them and communicating decisions to them. But this activity did not entail any theory that the local leaders were acting as the plenipotentiary representatives of their communities. Such a theory could only come about by adopting a clearcut conception of legal procuration. The chief innovation of thirteenth-century government is the growing use of such a conception in the tasks of politics.

Taking England as a concrete example, we may appreciate the introduction of representative theory by comparing the wording of two famous royal summonses, one at the beginning of the century and the other at its close. The first is King John's summons in 1213 to the sheriff of Oxfordshire (and presumably to the sheriffs of other counties) to arrange for the sending of 'four discreet men from your own county to us—to talk with us concerning the affairs of our kingdom'. The second is a writ of Edward I (1272–1307) in summons to the so-called Model Parliament of 1295. Here Edward orders chosen men from shires, towns and boroughs throughout England to present themselves at Westminster, bringing with them 'full and sufficient power (*plenam et sufficientem potestatem*) from their communities', so that, as the summons goes on, 'the business in hand may not be held up in any way through lack of such power'.

The difference between the type of assembly contemplated in each case emerges clearly. Edward I envisages a full-scale representative assembly, whose members will be able to bind the communities from which they come to whatever the general counsel of king and realm decides. There is no evidence that John was asking for any such representative body; in fact it seems very likely that he was merely seeking a way to collect reliable local information in the pattern of his Norman and Angevin predecessors from the days of Domesday Book onwards. The chief difference between the two summonses is marked by Edward I's requirement that delegates be furnished by their communities with *plena potestas*. It was this which made them real representatives of the corporate bodies to which they belonged.

Plena potestas is the pivotal conception of the representative system evolved by the Middle Ages and handed on to modern times. Its importance can hardly be exaggerated, yet it is only comparatively recently that its original significance in the development of representation has been made clear. Roman private law was already familiar with the useful arrangement whereby a principal in a legal suit might appoint an agent or proctor with full power to conduct the case on his behalf and to commit him to acceptance of the final judgement. This practice was especially useful in the case of corporate bodies, who would obviously find it impracticable to conduct their case in court for themselves. The medieval pioneers in adopting this practice were the canonists who began to mention *plena potestas* by name in the later twelfth century. There are no twelfth-century recorded cases of the use of *plena potestas* in secular law, but representation in this way was certainly in the air, encouraged by the growth of corporate associations in every walk of life.

63

The first clear political use of the formula comes from Italy, where in 1200 Innocent III ordered proctors from six cities in the March of Ancona, part of the Papacy's temporal dominions, to meet his Curia for consultation on various judicial, administrative and financial matters. Later, again in Italy, we know of a summons by Frederick II (1197–1250) in 1231 to different Italian cities to send to him proctors with full powers (*auctoritas* is the word used in this case) to give him advice and to accept his decisions.

It is not surprising that Italy, where Roman law had its deepest roots, should take the lead in applying to public law a technique originally designed for use in private legal actions. Nor is it a matter for wonder that the Papacy, the patron and promoter of the study of Romano-canonical law, should have been the first political authority to think of using proctorial representation as a system of government. But the system was acclimatized comparatively soon in other parts of western Europe, and by the end of the thirteenth century we find representative assemblies on a national basis becoming familiar in England, France and the Spanish kingdoms. It has indeed often been argued that Spain was first in the field with representative political assemblies during the twelfth century; but it has recently been demonstrated that there is no conclusive evidence that the twelfth-century Spanish assemblies had any real representative element about them.

The advantages to the king of a working system of corporate representation are clear enough. At a stroke he would be able to bypass all the long and wearisome negotiations with separate individuals and organizations and kill a good many birds of required consent with the one stone of a representative assembly. The principle of *plena potestas* would bind to all decisions reached at such an assembly even those members of a community who had previously been able to plead ignorance of, or lack of consent to, the measures agreed upon by the corporate body to which they belonged. Here more Roman law traditions were brought into play. The rule of majority

64

decisions as binding a whole community (even those who had voted against the majority) met the problem of individual dissidence within a corporate body. Meanwhile the Roman private law maxim of the delegated full powers of proctors to agree to a legal settlement even in the absence of their principals had, when applied to political representation, closed the door against attempts by a community to disclaim responsibility for agreements reached between its representatives and the central authority of the realm. The tag *Quod omnes tangit ab omnibus approbetur* (What concerns all, should be approved by all) was not an assertion of embryonic democracy so much as a device of the monarchy to obtain a guaranteed assent of the realm to its demands. Medieval representatives enjoyed no right to refuse their consent to royal policies. The spokesmen for a community might indeed attempt to petition the king to drop his demands for financial subsidies or to limit their amount. But the will of the monarch remained the last word; in this sense the royal prerogative was never seriously challenged. The medieval representative system was indeed the most refined example of what A. B. White, the American historian, described as 'self-government at the king's command', and it was appropriate that it should find its most lasting success in England, the country where such self-government had existed longer than elsewhere.

The government of the *Sacerdotium* was faced with the same administrative problems as that of the *Regnum*. The thirteenth century marked the peak of the concentration of power over the Church in the centralized authority of the Papacy. The Popes were now able to make their voices heard in appointing to high offices in the Church; indeed, with the introduction of the system of 'provisions' and 'reservations', they were often able to monopolize such appointments. Papal officials were able to circulate freely over western Europe, while at the Curia a vast bureaucratic organization, capable of dealing with all problems of Church administration and discipline, took shape. In keeping with this centralization the decretalists emphasized the legal supremacy of the Pope over the *Sacerdotium* and his rights to control the functions of the clerical hierarchy from top to bottom. Like the monarchical authority in the secular sphere, the canonists of the thirteenth century encouraged the reference of all types of legal problems and disputes to the Pope or his delegated officials, usually more expert and efficient in handling such problems than the local hierarchies.

The usual legal expression of this papal centralization was the theory of *plenitudo potestatis* (fulness of power) of the Pope. The phrase appears to have been first used by St. Bernard to describe the Pope's responsibility of ecclesiastical government. Its first official use in papal documents under Alexander III (1159–1181) refers to delegation of power to a papal Legate, parallel to the principle of *plena potestas* in civil and canon law. In the thirteenth century the character of the Pope's *potestas* as agent for the Christian community was interpreted so as to give him a practically absolute position in Church government and even, as we shall see later, in secular affairs also. The Pope was thought by most decretalists to enjoy the same absolute sovereignty over the *Sacerdotium* as the *Lex Regia* had granted to the Emperor in secular affairs. The scope of papal authority could be limited only by explicit provisions of divine and natural law and even there some canonists held that the Pope might exercise a dispensing power. In such theories of Papal supremacy the position of the general council was seriously depreciated, most decretalists holding that conciliar legislation possessed binding force only when underwritten by the Papacy.

It has recently been pointed out that the thirteenth-century tendency towards a centralized papal *plenitudo potestatis* advanced side by side with another legal concept which the decretalists did much to explore but which in the long run was bound to clash with an absolute monarchy. This was the concept of the *Sacerdotium* as being composed of various corporations, each with its own carefully articulated organiza-

66

tion and representative officials. The corporation idea corresponded perfectly to the facts of the practical situation of the sacerdotal hierarchy below the Pope in the thirteenth century. We may fairly apply to the *Sacerdotium* as a whole Sir Maurice Powicke's description of its English branch: '—a sensitive and quarrelsome organism of vested interests and of rights rooted in custom and privilege.'

As the relations between these interests were largely determined by litigation it was essential that each group concerned should possess an unassailable legal standing and should therefore be regarded as a corporate body, capable of asserting rights which its individual members would have been legally incapable of vindicating for themselves. The problems of consent and counsel involved were thrashed out by the decretalists by methods reminiscent of contemporary secular processes of representation. In particular the legal status of a bishop in relation to the clergy of his diocese and especially his cathedral chapter underwent a significant change; he was now regarded as a proctor representing the rights of the clerical corporation of which he was the head. An extreme theory went as far as to regard the chapter which elected the bishop as the source of his episcopal authority.

How were these ideas applied to the Church as a whole? Some thirteenth-century thinkers, notably Pope Innocent IV (1243–1254), himself a distinguished canonist, thought it perfectly possible to reconcile the idea of the whole Church as a corporation with papal *plenitudo potestatis*. They did so by arguing that all the powers of a corporation were vested in its head, in this case the Papacy. Here again we meet an echo of the absolutist interpretation of Roman law. By contrast, the greatest of the decretalists, Hostiensis (*d.* 1271), believed that the authority of a corporation was also shared by its members. In his application of this belief to the *Sacerdotium* he not only claimed for the College of Cardinals, to which he belonged, a share in papal *plenitudo potestatis* (though this need not necessarily mean that he believed that the Pope could not act without the Cardinals) but also held that in case of emergency a general council, representing the whole body of the faithful, could step in as the final authority in the Church.

A little later in the century two Parisian University Masters, Henry of Ghent (*d.* 1293) and Godfrey of Fontaines (*d.* 1303), speaking from a theological rather than a canonistic viewpoint, argued that papal authority must always be exercised in conformity with the established laws of the Church and its traditional channels of government, the bishops. Godfrey went a stage further when he hinted at the possibility of the entire 'community of the faithful' being qualified to pass condemnations of heresy. He did not, however, specify whether this communal judgement was to be expressed through a representative general council or not.

Monarchical and papal centralization, corporative and representative theories, were taking the thirteenth century away from the earlier medieval feudal world. The new tendencies squared ill with the patristic traditional theory of political power as a mere remedy for sin, a regrettable necessity which would not have existed but for the fall of man. It is not surprising that a philosophy which included a more positive outlook on social and political life should have rapidly gained ground; at this juncture Aristotle's political philosophy was reintroduced to the west.

So far as the earlier Middle Ages had indulged in philosophy at all it had tended to be a form of Neoplatonism, chiefly as interpreted by St. Augustine and with the boundaries with theology none too closely defined. The general trend of this Christian wisdom of the dark ages was to depreciate both the material world and unaided human reason. Some of Aristotle's logical works were known through a Latin translation by Boethius (480–525), but the mass of Aristotle's philosophy was more familiar to the Islamic civilization than it was to the Christian world. When Aristotle returned in the late twelfth and early thirteenth centuries he did so accompanied by the commentaries of Moslem philosophers such as

Avicenna (980–1037) and Averroes (1126–1198). The *Politics* itself was one of the last of Aristotle's works to be known; it was translated direct from the Greek about 1260 by William of Moerbeke, a friend of St. Thomas Aquinas.

The notion of politics as a separate branch of knowledge was not unfamiliar before the thirteenth century but it was the direct influence of Aristotle's thought which enabled medieval political theory to come of age. Now for the first time since the fall of the Roman Empire, western Christian thinkers came face to face with the possibility that political society was of value in its own right. For Aristotle, the political commonwealth was 'a creation of nature' and man was 'by nature a political animal'; indeed it was only by participation in the life of his political community that an individual man could fully participate in the good life, the positive purpose for which the political community exists. One can imagine the excitement and (in some cases) alarm with which the thinkers of the thirteenth century must have discovered this revolutionary theory. If Aristotle was to be taken at his word, the old conception of a unified Christian religious-political commonwealth must inevitably be modified to make room for a clear field of autonomy for the secular community. How far could such a modification be carried without threatening the dogmas of Christian orthodoxy?

The question did not arise in political science only. The re-entry of Aristotle had posed it in every realm of Christian thought. In the sphere of Christian wisdom, philosophy, represented by the new Aristoteleanism, had begun to claim its autonomy from theology. Sometimes the claim was made in an exaggeratedly radical form, as in the case of the so-called Latin Averroists who, reading Aristotle in the light of his greatest Arab commentator Averroes (1126–1198), deduced from him such theories as that of the unity of the human intellect and hence the denial of reality to the individual soul. Their argument that orthodoxy could be saved by making a sharp separation between the truths of faith and those of reason was viewed with understandable suspicion by the ecclesiastical authorities and the condemnations in which the Averroists were involved threw discredit on the Aristotelean movement as a whole. The century holds numerous records of papal and episcopal prohibitions of the general study of Aristotle's writings.

Some Catholic thinkers, by contrast, saw nothing impossible in the reconciliation of Aristotle with orthodoxy. St. Albert the Great (c. 1206–1280) had attempted the task in a rather discursive manner but it was left to his pupil, St. Thomas Aquinas (1224–1274), to carry out the first and most impressive synthesis of Christianity and Aristotelean philosophy. Full justice to Thomas's new departure in scholastic thought is hardly done when it is presented exclusively in terms of the relationship between the Christian Faith and Aristotle. These, fundamental though they were, did not provide the only ingredients of Thomism. The older medieval philosophical tradition of Neoplatonism was respectfully pressed into service by Thomas whenever he needed it and so in the legal and political portions of his writings were the systems of Roman and canon law. He had not indeed a direct knowledge of the civil law; as a priest he would have been forbidden in any case to study it. But he seems to have acquired an accurate understanding of its principles and more important maxims through the medium of canon law, with which he had much more than a nodding acquaintance.

To treat St. Thomas's political theory as a separate field of study is almost as artificial as it is to treat St. Augustine's as such. Thomas wrote no complete treatise on politics, apart from a commentary on Aristotle's *Politics*, and his remarks on the social and political order have to be extracted from the main structure of his philosophical and theological works. These remarks, however, when put together, give us a broad picture of a legal and political system which may be ambiguous when it descends to details (as it hardly ever does) but which in its general *ethos* represents perhaps the most balanced presentation of all the elements present in the medieval political tradition after the Aristotelean revival. St. Thomas's political comments are contained primarily in his great *Summa Theologica* and to a secondary degree in his *De Regimine Principum*, a manual on the art of government for the King of Cyprus; neither was ever finished by St. Thomas. The two works are written in quite different styles. The *De Regimine* is a straightforward piece of didactic writing, while the *Summa* is a masterpiece of Scholastic dialectical technique, divided and subdivided into parts, articles and questions, in the framework of which the argument is conducted on the pattern of the academic disputation: assertion, objection, answer to objections and conclusion. Nowhere is St. Thomas, for all his Aristoteleanism, *ex professo* a political thinker. When he touches on political problems he deals with them as parentheses in the exposition of his main theological line of thought. Thus his definition of political authority in the *Summa* is contained in a discussion of man before the fall, while other political matters come in for mention in Thomas's examination of various virtues and vices. This relegation of political science to a footnote may seem strange to our modern liking for specialization, but for St. Thomas it was the logical and obvious course. He was after all a theologian first and last, a true Dominican carrying out his study in the service of God and the-Church. As such it was quite natural that the study of human political life should be but a part, and that not the most important part, of his general theological system. There was no room for tension or dualism between secular and spiritual issues in the mind of St. Thomas. The careful unity of his presentation is a clear reminder of the attraction which the old ideal of a unified Christian society still exerted in the thirteenth century.

This does not mean that Thomas wished to swallow up all political government in a theocracy, any more than it meant that he wanted to make philosophy nothing but a pacemaker for the benefit of theology. His attitude in both instances can

71

best be summed up in his own words: 'Nature is not destroyed by grace but perfected by it.' Human reason, far from being incompatible with the supernatural gifts of God, achieves its full stature and power with their assistance. The corollary to this is that the present condition of corrupted human nature, sad as it is, is not a total perversion of human nature but rather an incomplete reflection of what God intended it to be and as it actually was before the fall. Even in the state of innocence, Thomas declares, there would have to be differences between individuals in age and sex if in nothing else. Thomas himself would go further and assert that differences in intellectual capacity would also have existed and that therefore some individuals would have been better qualified for leadership than others. The use of such leadership for the common good would have been necessary even without the fall; here Thomas tacitly parts company with the old patristic tradition of the conventional character of political authority. St. Thomas regards political life as an essential feature of man's original and therefore natural condition.

The concept of political society is thus detached from its previous connection in Christian thought with original sin, its consequences and remedies, and hence from any inherent connection with the economy of redemption and the Church, the channel through which the benefits of redemption are conveyed. Thomas prefers to associate political society with the economy of creation; for him it is part of nature as God made it and would therefore have existed if man had never sinned and thereby made redemption and the Church necessary. The result of this was that Thomas, in effect, altered the definition, current since Augustine, of true political society as inseparably bound up with a Christian Commonwealth. Political society now has its own right to existence and does not depend for its legitimacy on its connection with the Church. For the first time in medieval thought we meet something resembling the modern idea of the State, and it is interesting that it should be in the Italy of St. Thomas's time that the first examples of use of the term in its modern sense are found.

It would of course be absurd to maintain that Thomas laicized the State. For him it was part of the economy of creation and owed its significance to its place in God's eternal plan for all the stages of universal being. It was to this plan that all patterns of political society should be referred if they were to fulfil their true purpose. Like the canonists and civilians Thomas finds the ultimate meaning of political activity to be in its conformity to a higher universal law.

Law for Thomas had two distinct but complementary meanings, which he indicated by his use of two Latin words, *lex* and *ius*. *Lex* is defined in Thomas's own terms as 'any rule and measure of actions as a result of which any person is induced to act or restrained from acting', while *ius* is described as 'a correct relationship between one action and another according to a mutually applicable standard'. In the first case law is looked on as a conscious enactment by some reasoned will, 'a certain command of the practical reason in the supreme authority which rules a fully developed community'. In the second case the more passive sense of the concept 'law' is in mind; St. Thomas uses *ius* to describe the natural inclinations and conditions of the various parts of creation, functioning together to fulfil the purposes destined for them by God. He also applies the term to comparatively artificial relationships, such as agreements among a group of individuals to submit to certain legal, economic and political standards. From this angle St. Thomas's approach to government and its origins bears some resemblance to a Social Contract theory.

The motivating forces of law in the sense of creative rational activity are reason and will and its object is the common good. The co-ordination of individual actions towards this common good is the function 'either of the whole community or of some person acting in the place of the whole community'. St. Thomas describes this representative agent as the 'public person who has charge over the whole community'. Such

73

an authority must have at his disposal the coercive power to enforce the laws recommended by his reason. Thomas draws all the strings of his argument together when he defines law as 'any enactment of reason directed towards the common good and promulgated by the authority which is in charge of the community'. Nothing could illustrate better than this succinct definition the skill with which Thomas combined Aristotelean philosophical concepts with the Natural Law tradition already familiar to the west. Aristotle's influence may be seen in the division between the material cause of legislation (the enactment itself), the formal cause (the rational motive behind the enactment), the efficient cause (the legislative authority) and the final cause (the common good). The old Natural Law tradition is implicit in the emphasis on reason and promulgation in the definition.

St. Thomas in fact has no difficulty in incorporating the traditional concept of Natural Law into his system and he makes use of it in relation to both *lex* and *ius*. His double definition of law forms the basis of his description of the eternal law by which God rules the whole universe, the law which is the foundation for all other divisions of law, whether human or divine. Eternal law is 'the rational guidance of created things on the part of God'; to non-rational creatures this is manifested by their implanted instincts which urge them to fulfil the role in creation allotted to them by God.

Even man in part of his nature falls into this non-rational category; his instincts towards self-preservation and the perpetuation of the species are not conditioned by any consciously directing rational force. But by virtue of his possession of reason, his distinguishing quality, man has the chance to co-operate in the working of the eternal law. This 'participation in the eternal law by rational creatures' is for St. Thomas a satisfactory definition of the natural law, while human or positive law is a particular application of the general rational principles taught by the natural law.

The term 'positive law', which was to have an important

future before it, had been known in French legal and philosophical circles of the twelfth century, by way of Chalcidius's fourth-century Latin translation of Plato's *Timaeus*. In the early thirteenth century it had penetrated into the legal school at Bologna and this may have been the *milieu* from which Thomas received the term. He seems to use this concept of *ius positivum* to include both the legal divisions known to Roman law as the *ius gentium* and the *ius civile* respectively. The *ius gentium* is defined on familiar lines as 'those precepts which are derived from the natural law as conclusions are from principles': Thomas cites social activities such as buying and selling as examples and he is able to find, like the civilians and canonists, justification for institutions such as property and slavery. The *ius civile* is derived from the natural law by 'a process of particular application'. In both cases the natural law is in a sense changed by addition and other changes in it may be made by legitimate relaxation or dispensation from its provisions. Such changes are not against the spirit of the natural law; on the contrary, they are actuated by it for the rational purpose of furthering the common good of the community. If they were not, they would not merit the title of law at all, since they would have cut away the base on which all human law stands. All such unjust laws should be resisted by those subject to them, provided such resistance does not itself bring about a still greater evil.

Human positive law itself may *a fortiori* be modified when the occasion requires. The modification may be affected either by a conscious change carried out by direct legislative authority or by the more gradual pressure of custom. Thomas emphasizes that the first method should only be resorted to when there is clear evidence that the common good requires the law to be changed. The rational character of customary changes in law is defended by the argument that such changes in action are just as much motivated by the reasoned will as are the written changes of statutory law. St. Thomas's respect for customary law is, of course, in line with Germanic tradition; but

75

it is also in keeping with Aristotle's preference for unwritten law as less liable to abuse. The consensus of public practice in a free community (i.e. one which acknowledges no feudal superior) is sufficient to establish a customary practice as law. Even in a community which has an overlord customary practice may become valid law if it is tolerated 'by those who have to enforce the law on the community'; in such a case the overlord is presumed to give his consent, even if it is not made explicit. St. Thomas may here be carrying a brief for the Italian towns of his own day who were all making extensive constitutional changes even though still officially subject to the Empire.

The common good for St. Thomas is the touchstone by which to judge the validity of all modifications of law. But what does he mean by the common good and how does it affect the individual's relation to the State? From one angle his answer might be construed as giving the State a kind of totalitarian priority over the individual, much as Plato had done in his *Republic*. Thus Thomas argues that individual goodness can only be judged by its contribution to the goodness of the community; 'since a man is part of the city, it is impossible for any man to be good, unless he is properly in conformity with the common good'. The common good is not merely the sum total of the individual goods of those composing the community, as nineteenth-century Benthamism was to hold. For Thomas the difference between common and individual good is one not only of quantity but also of kind; in stressing this he is again in close conformity with Aristotle.

On the other hand the fact that St. Thomas was a Christian thinker prevented him from regarding the individual as a mere transitory portion of the State. The individual after all possessed an immortal soul with a destiny higher than that of any earthly community; it was in defence of personal immortality that the Church had condemned Averroism's theory of the unity of the intellect in the human species. We find St. Thomas therefore qualifying his assertion of individual subordination

76

to the common good by pointing out that the unity of the political community is one of order and hierarchy rather than a strictly organic unity.

His best explanation of his position is found in his *Commentary on Aristotle's Nicomachean Ethics*; in his introduction to this he says that analogies for the type of unity he has in mind may be provided by an army or by men engaged in rowing a boat. In either case the parts which form the unity 'can have a mode of action which is not the mode of action of the whole'. Similarly, when discussing human law in the *Summa Theologica*, he declares that 'the common good is made up of many parts' and that consequently the law must cater for legitimate individual interests. The same concern for the individual is reflected in Thomas's concession of the right to resist laws 'whose weight may be unequally distributed throughout the community, even if they may be intended for the common good'.

So far we have been examining Thomas's views on the aims and duties of political government. But what of the actual composition of the government? Here we are confronted with what to many commentators has seemed a contradiction. In *De regimine Principum* Thomas speaks decisively in favour of monarchy as the best form of government. He backs up his opinion by various arguments, some of them rather far-fetched for modern taste. Not only is monarchy the form of government best calculated to secure unity of direction in policy, and the most like God's method of ruling the universe; but even the fact that the bees are ruled on a monarchical system is cited as additional corroboration. Monarchy is for Thomas the most natural form of government. He admits that its perversion in the tyranny of one man is the worst possible political system, although in another section of the book he rather inconsistently maintains that abuse of democratic government leads to more harmful consequences than an individual tyranny. In one portion of the *Summa Theologica* Thomas puts forward another argument for monarchy when

77

he says that the more reducible to unity a government is, the better can it inspire unity in those it governs. As nothing can be more reducible to unity than a single individual, it follows that monarchy is the best type of government.

When we turn to another section of the *Summa* we find an apparently contradictory view. Here, during a discussion of the Old Testament monarchical system of the Jews, Thomas says that a mixed form of government, incorporating features from monarchy, aristocracy and democracy, is the best. He has in mind not only Aristotle's polity as described in the *Politics* but also the even more compelling authority of Scripture itself, which recorded the divine institution of such a mixed type of constitution for Israel. A little later in the same passage Thomas, while conceding that an uncorrupted monarchy is the ideal form of government, is as sceptical as Lord Acton on the possibility of an absolute ruler's ability to resist the temptations of power.

What are we to make of these seemingly inconsistent pronouncements? Some modern commentators have tried to cut the Gordian knot by declaring that none of the *De Regimine Principum* is Thomas's authentic work. But this is a counsel of despair and does not in any case solve the problem of the differing statements within the *Summa Theologica*. An answer to this baffling conundrum may be suggested if we examine exactly what Thomas says in the reference to a mixed polity. The definition he gives of the aristocratic ingredient in the mixture makes clear that this element is subordinate to the monarch, while by democracy he means that 'the rulers can be chosen from among the people, and the election of rulers is the prerogative of the people'.

All this still leaves the executive and legislative control of the community in the hands of the monarch, though he may work through aristocratic advisers and owe his original elevation to election by the *populus*. The mention of the *populus* raises the legitimate reflection whether Thomas may not have had in mind Roman law's doctrine of the popular

derivation of authority; if he had, this would not be inconsistent with holding that the governmental power of the
monarchy was absolute. Elsewhere, in his *Commentary on
St. Paul's Epistle to the Romans*, Thomas talks of the origin of
the State as being 'a kind of pact between king and people'.
So his derivation of monarchy from popular election in the
Summa need be no more incompatible with support of an
absolute monarchy than are the theories of popular sovereignty
embodied in the Roman law of the days of the absolute
Empire. Perhaps after all we may be led to conclude that there
is no fundamental inconsistency in Thomas's various statements if we try to look at them in his own terms and not to
allow our own modern antitheses of absolutism and constitutional democracy to confuse the issue.

The rebirth of the Aristotelean conception of the natural
character of the State was developed with enthusiasm by other
thinkers of the later thirteenth and early fourteenth centuries.
Peter of Auvergne (*d.* 1302), in his commentary on Aristotle's
Politics, subtracted revealed Christianity from his discussion
of the State and described a priestly hierarchy teaching a
natural religion. Peter's approach is close to that taken later
by Thomas More (1478–1535) in his *Utopia*; yet Peter was no
less orthodox than More. Remigio di Girolami (1235–1319),
the Florentine Dominican who was pupil of St. Thomas
Aquinas and teacher of Dante, went furthest of all when he
said: 'If you are not a citizen you are not a man, because a
man is naturally a civil animal.' The trend of the new philosophy towards a totalitarian view of the State received no
more striking expression than in the words of the same
thinker: 'The whole is more fully united to the part than the
part is to itself.'

The feudal conception of personal loyalty to an overlord
was transmuted by these thinkers into a theory of loyalty to
the community as a whole and of individual self-effacement
before the common good. The old classical ideal of 'dying for
the fatherland' received fresh currency, while some writers

went as far as to appropriate ecclesiastical terminology for the State's benefit by talking about the mystical body of the secular political community. The result of this fever of re-discovery of pre-Christian ideas on politics was to face the former Christian politico-religious ideal of a Christian Commonwealth, existant in its two branches of *Sacerdotium* and *Regnum*, with a potent and ultimately incompatible rival—the self-sufficient organism of the State.

CHAPTER VI

DESIGNS FOR A WORLD MONARCHY

THE trend towards transforming the *Regnum* from a branch
of the Christian Commonwealth into an autonomous corporate
body, the State, would clearly find opposition from the *Sacerdotium* and particularly the Papacy. As if in reaction to the
threat, the Papacy began to claim for itself, in its capacity as
head of the *Sacerdotium,* direct monarchical authority over the
whole of Christian society. In effect the thirteenth-century
papalists metamorphozed the old Christian Commonwealth
into a State on the new model but under papal monarchy and
with the secular rulers degraded to the rank of subordinate
assistants to the papal world government. The clashes of the
thirteenth and fourteenth centuries between the Papacy and
the secular power were the inevitable accompaniments of the
Papacy's attempt to establish its claim to be the State above all
States.

It was on the canonists that there fell the brunt of the
theoretical battle. We have already noticed how, about the
turn of the twelfth and thirteenth centuries, it seems probable
that they passed to a novel use of the important concept of the
gladius materialis, which they now took to imply secular
political authority as such and not merely the Church's
coercive power. The English canonist, Alanus, writing during
Innocent III's pontificate, seems on the whole to claim that
the Papacy possessed *plenitudo potestatis* in the temporal
sphere.

Innocent III never made any such explicit official claim for
himself but it is true that his diplomatic policy, particularly
with regard to the Empire, might well amount to such a claim
in practice, given the almost unlimited scope of political

intervention which he would be able to vindicate *pro ratione peccati*. It was also Innocent III who initiated the use of the title Vicar of Christ to describe the papal office, thereby laying the foundations of the most telling theological argument for papalist political claims. The conception of the Pope as Christ's Vicar was linked by Innocent with the Pope's consequent succession to Christ's function of kingship, though Innocent's characteristic theoretical moderation saw in this succession no more than the justification for government of the Papal States and for his feudal overlordship of various secular kingdoms. It was left for theologians later in the century to deduce the theory of direct power for the Papacy in temporal affairs (or, as it is now often called, the hierocratic theory) from the Vicar of Christ conception. Robert Grosseteste (*d.* 1253), like Alanus, an Englishman, seems to have been the first theologian to argue explicitly for the Pope's direct power, and it is significant that he lays much stress on the Pope's inheritance of Christ's regal prerogatives, though he does not actually use the Vicar of Christ title. It is also perhaps not without interest that this pioneer of the direct power theory should also have been a pioneer in the diffusion of Aristotelean philosophy; Grosseteste directed a translation of the *Nicomachean Ethics* into Latin. Indeed the Aristotelean metaphysical idea (as set forth in *De Anima*) of the subordination of the human substance as a whole to the soul as its directing force provided the hierocratic papalist theologians with the argument that the *Sacerdotium* as director of the soul, could also direct the sphere of material secular affairs.

The position of St. Thomas Aquinas in this matter has been the subject of much difference of opinion. The relevant data has to be pieced together from incidental references in various works of Aquinas written at different stages of his intellectual career. The earliest comes from his youthful *Commentary on the Sentences of Peter Lombard*.

In a short discussion on the relationship between the spiritual and secular powers St. Thomas says that each has its

82

own proper sphere, in which it is to be obeyed by the other. Had he stopped there he might have been safely labelled as a follower of the Gelasian tradition. But in fact he went on to add the qualification: 'Unless indeed the spiritual and secular powers are both held by the same person, as they are by the Pope, who stands supreme over each power, spiritual and secular, by the disposition of (Christ) Who is both Priest and King, Priest for ever after the order of Melchisedech, King of kings and Lord of lords, Whose power shall not be taken away and Whose Kingdom shall never see corruption. Amen.'

Later commentators have often put forward a minimal interpretation of this statement; on their interpretation St. Thomas would be referring to the Pope's temporal rule over the Papal States in central Italy. If this argument is accepted it is still possible to regard Thomas as adhering to the dualist Gelasian position. But do his words really bear such an interpretation? If so precise a thinker as Aquinas had intended merely to refer to the Pope's Italian dominions he could quite easily have said so clearly; as it is, it is perhaps more faithful to his meaning to take his words as they stand and to admit that he seems here to be upholding direct papal temporal power in the widest sense. This supposition is strengthened by his reference to the Kingship of Christ and His eternal *Regnum*, concepts which were used by other writers of the time to buttress undoubtedly hierocratic arguments. It is hard to believe that the impressive doxology with which Thomas closes is merely intended to round off a demonstration of the legitimacy of papal power over a few territories in central Italy.

In the *De Regimine Principum* Thomas speaks of 'the high priest, the successor of Peter, the Vicar of Christ, the Roman Pontiff' as being the authority in charge of man's final end and hence as occupying a position of superiority over those authorities concerned with his subordinate ends. It would be rash to assert that this may be definitely read as a clear support for the theory of direct power; yet it seems to fit in better with such a theory than with any other. The only other passage in which St. Thomas speaks of papal relationship to the secular power is in his *Quaestiones Quodlibetales*, but his reference here is to the Papacy's feudal overlordship of certain kingdoms and hence brings no clarification to his position on the main issue of direct power.

Even if it is accepted as more likely that St. Thomas was a supporter of the hierocratic theory it must be acknowledged that at any rate he is among its more cautious exponents. This may best be appreciated by comparing him with other hierocratic writers of the century. It is when we do this that we realize how strongly entrenched in official papalist ideology the theory became during the thirteenth century.

The decisive steps towards its adoption seem to have been taken by the two great canonist Popes Gregory IX (1227–1241) and Innocent IV (1243–1254) during their conflict with Frederick II, whose bid to obtain control of Italy they withstood with ultimate success. Final victory over Frederick's Hohenstauffen descendants was, however, only achieved at the price of installing a French dynasty in Naples and accepting a degree of French control over the Papacy's diplomatic policy. In a letter of October 23, 1236 (*Si memoriam beneficiorum*), to Frederick, Gregory quoted the Donation of Constantine as a proof of acknowledgement by the secular power that (to use Gregory's words) 'as the Prince of the Apostles governed the empire of priesthood and souls in the whole world, so he should also reign over material and corporeal affairs throughout the whole world'.

Innocent IV staked his claim to direct power still more forcibly and fully both in official pronouncements as Pope and in a more private capacity as commentator on canon law. He contended that the Pope is the *iudex ordinarius* (highest competent judge) of all men. This papal jurisdiction extended, according to Innocent, not only to Christians, but even to infidels, though Innocent conceded that the heathen could not

84

be deprived of their possessions without good cause, as they held them by the natural law. In keeping with this general theory Innocent declared that the Donation of Constantine was nothing other than the handing over to the Papacy of the *de facto* possession of what it already held *de iure*. Innocent put his theory into drastic practice when he proclaimed Frederick to be deposed in 1245. He did so on the ground that outside the Church 'no authority is ordained by God'.

Hostiensis took a still more extreme view. He held that the Pope's supreme control over all temporal things entitled him to deprive pagans of their territory or property if he thought fit. Hostiensis's opinion on this point is an interesting example of the Christian imperialism of the crusading age, though the reconquest of the Holy Land was itself a lost cause at the time he was writing. Like Innocent, Hostiensis argued that the Pope possessed complete authority over the secular power, particularly over the Empire, though the Papacy might not always in practice see fit to exercise such authority. Hostiensis's belief in papal *plenitudo potestatis* in temporal affairs is all the more striking in view of his tendency, as we have seen, to limit the scope of papal authority in the internal government of the *Sacerdotium*.

The most comprehensively argued statements of the hierocratic theory were called forth by the famous conflict between Pope Boniface VIII (1294–1303) and Philip IV of France (1285–1314), at the turn of the thirteenth and fourteenth centuries. The conflict, beginning as a clash of secular and ecclesiastical legal systems over the issues of clerical immunity and taxation, became a fight to the finish between Pope and King and ended in the political defeat and humiliation of the Papacy. The transfer of the papal seat of residence by the pliable French Pope, Clement V (1305–1314), to French-controlled Avignon, where it remained until 1378, was a not unnatural postscript. From one angle, then, the outcome of the Bonifacian struggle may be considered as the collapse of the theory of direct power before the adverse logic of events. But

85

the very intensity of the conflict impelled the supporters of the Papacy to enunciate arguments even more radical than those of Innocent IV and Hostiensis.

The canonists, who had set the pace throughout the thirteenth century, were now left behind by a remarkable group of theologians who came mainly from the Augustinian Order of Friars. By comparison the public utterances of Boniface VIII himself remain moderate. The famous Bull *Unam Sanctam* (1302) certainly argues for direct power; Boniface uses the 'two swords' theory and the hierarchical ordering of the universe to prove his point. But the final pronouncement that 'it is altogether necessary to salvation for every human creature to be subject to the Roman Pontiff' need not mean more than a claim for spiritual supremacy.

There is no possibility of a moderate interpretation for the treatise of Giles of Rome (*c.* 1246–1316), *De Potestate Ecclesiastica*. From first to last the work is an attempt to draw the most rigorously extreme deductions from the various metaphysical and (if the word may be used) sociological arguments produced by the author. In the first of the three books of which the work is composed Giles deals with the general problem of the Papacy's relationship to the secular power. In conformity with the new demands of the controversy with the French Crown, all Giles's arguments are directed towards the *Regnum* as such and the preoccupation of thirteenth-century papalists with the specific question of the Empire is forgotten.

Underlying all the familiar arguments used by Giles lies a definite flavour of St. Augustine's philosophy of human society. Giles frankly disagrees with the cherished Thomist-Aristotelean principle of the natural character of political communities; for him it is only ecclesiastical sanction and approbation which raises these communities above their original title-deeds of brigandage and usurpation. The resemblance to the *City of God* is clear; like Augustine, Giles cannot grant the quality of justice to any State which is not Christian.

In his second book Giles enters realms of which Augustine can hardly have dreamed. He proceeds to argue that the validity of any ownership of private property (*dominium*) depends, not on natural inheritance or acquisition but on loyal membership of the Church. It is this argument, the so-called *dominium* theory, which constitutes the real novelty of Giles's position.

The word *dominium* had been created by medieval Latin to express the feudal conception of ownership. Giles takes it to mean the proprietorial capacity in general and holds that there can be no true *dominium* without the justice which only the Church, by its supernatural channels of grace, can impart. Thus every rightful owner of property must be a baptized person, for baptism alone can give him the *sine qua non* of Church membership. It is no use to argue that property descends by carnal inheritance from one's father and ancestors; to hold it lawfully the proprietor must be not only *generatus* ('born') according to the flesh but *regeneratus* ('reborn') spiritually by grace. Human birth does indeed give the initial qualification for inheritance, but that qualification must be completed and ratified by the Church. But even after baptism it is possible for an individual to forfeit temporarily or permanently by mortal sin or excommunication his member-ship of the Church. So Giles's theory boils down to the con-clusion that no one can rightfully possess any property unless he is in a state of grace. No wonder that Giles himself sums up the consequence of his argument in the striking phrase: 'The Church is more the owner of thy property than thou thyself art.' Significantly enough Giles here uses the same sort of language as a thinker like Remigio di Girolami was using at the same period about the State.

To meet the objection that his theory means a virtual nullification of natural human rights Giles makes a distinction between what he describes as two forms of *dominium*. One form, the individual and secular, is only a partial and inferior derivation from the other, the universal *dominium* which the

Church alone possesses. Giles links this with the more extreme interpretation of the theory of the two swords. In effect Giles's explanation can have been but cold comfort for the secular power, for it still places ultimate and absolute sovereignty and ownership fairly and squarely in the hands of the Church and hence of the Papacy.

James of Viterbo (*d.* 1308) belonged, like Giles, to the Augustinian Order of Friars, and wrote his treatise *De Regimine Christiano* contemporaneously with Giles's own. But James is more definitely Aristotelean in his arguments. No papalist writer betrays more clearly than he the preoccupation to show that the Church itself is an all-inclusive, self-sufficient State according to Aristotelean requirements.

He begins by defining the *Regnum* as the highest form of human society. In doing so James, in common with other medieval Aristoteleans, extends the meaning of Aristotle's unit of the city-state to a wider territorial connotation. One would guess that the Greek philosopher himself would have regarded this development with suspicion; the medieval territorial monarchy would have seemed to him far too large to fit his conception of a true political community. But for James and his contemporaries it was clear that the *Regnum* was the 'perfect society' in the Aristotelean sense. Hence his task as a papalist controversialist was to prove that the Church is in fact the highest and oniy complete form of *Regnum* and that compared to it the secular *Regnum* is a partial and incomplete manifestation.

Following Aristotle's principle that the later development of any organism marks a higher stage of its existence (the acorn grows into the oak, the child into the man), James argues that the chronological lateness of the Church by comparison to the secular *Regnum* shows that the former is, philosophically speaking, superior to the latter. In any case, he goes on, the Church has all the distinguishing marks of a true *Regnum*; it possesses unity under a supreme authority with power to inflict legal sanctions and it has as its aim the sharing of the good life among its members. In fact the Church may lay claim to be the only perfect *Regnum*, because it alone is based on grace whereas secular *regna* are based on nature and are therefore inadequate owing to original sin. Just as individual fallen man needs the divine grace of revelation to supplement the deficiencies of his vitiated nature, so the secular *Regnum* needs sanctification by the Church in order to realize its full natural potentialities. 'All human power,' says James, 'is imperfect and unformed unless it be formed and perfected by the spiritual power.'

The position of the Papacy, as controller of this perfect church-state, is put at the highest possible level by James. The Pope possesses the most perfect form of royal as well as of priestly power. James even goes as far as to say that the Pope's royal power is higher in dignity than his priestly power, because priesthood is an office of mediation whereas kingship is one of absolute authority. There could be no better proof of the determination of the papalist hierocrats to rob the secular *Regnum* of its own weapons and to seize for the *Sacerdotium* all the attributes of the new concept of the State. The story of Boniface VIII's own appearance in the imperial purple during the Holy Year of 1300 may be apocryphal, but it is a correct symbolic expression of what the dominant school of papal apologists was claiming for the Papacy.

While James's conclusions are as extreme as Giles's his method of arriving at them is not based on a series of challenging syllogisms, as is Giles's habit. To get to his destination he employs an interesting combination of the at-first-sight incompatible Augustinian and Aristotelean political traditions. His definition of the ecclesiastical as well as of the secular *Regnum* is based on Aristotelean categories while his discussion of the relationship between them makes use of St. Augustine's key-idea of the secular State's incompleteness without the grace which can only be given by the Church.

The hierocratic case did not go unanswered, even by members of the *Sacerdotium*. Remigio di Girolami in his still unedited treatise *Contra falsos ecclesiae professores* argued that the authority of the Church in temporal matters could only be exercised 'indirectly'; one would expect this attitude from so vigorous an exponent of the claims of the State as Remigio. A more immediately influential writer was another Dominican, the French John of Paris (*d.* 1306), whose *De potestate regia et papali* was written during the Bonifacian controversy as a counterblast to the onslaughts of Giles of Rome and James of Viterbo. John's treatise, however, is more than a blow-by-blow refutation of his papalist opponents. It is a full-scale attempt to examine positively both the relations between *Regnum* and *Sacerdotium* and the internal constitution of the *Sacerdotium*. John casts his net of erudition very widely; his debt to Aristotle has long been recognized, but it has recently been shown that he was well abreast of the canonistic trends of his time and that his own work in turn did much to influence later generations of canonist writers.

John is no extremist; he does not wish, like the Spiritual Franciscans, that the Church should abandon all its temporalities. He does however want it to recognize that it holds such temporalities by the gift of secular authority and can hence advance no far-reaching claims to *plenitudo potestatis*. In opposition to James of Viterbo he argues that the *Regnum*, as the highest form of natural society, can be fully perfect in a strictly natural sense without the necessity of sanctification by the Church. John makes a sharp distinction between the spheres of grace and nature and accuses the papalists of obscuring this distinction. On the other hand, he himself does not confine the care of spiritual affairs solely to the Church. The *Regnum* has as its objective the common good, which of necessity includes the encouragement of citizens to lead a virtuous life and hence impinges to some extent on the sphere of the spiritual.

John does not follow this line of thought very far but it is easy to see how such a theory could later be used as a weapon

90

by advocates of the dominance of the secular authority over the Church. While admitting that the *Sacerdotium* is qualitatively superior to the *Regnum* because it has the higher goal, he contends that this does not entitle the *Sacerdotium* to claim supremacy in the *Regnum's* own sphere. John does not make absolute this vetoing of interference by either power in the other's sphere; he concedes that there may arise cases where it may become lawful for either authority to take action in the other's sphere if negligence or misgovernment makes this necessary.

John allows neither to the Papacy nor to the secular monarchy any absolute right of ownership over their subjects' property, although the monarchical authority in both *Sacerdotium* and *Regnum* has the right to judge disputes about private property and to dispense the goods pertaining to its own public office. It is not surprising that John rejects the idea that the Papacy has direct universal temporal power; what is novel is the reasoning he adopts for his conclusion. For the first time for several centuries a writer takes the bold step of cutting through the complicated knot of disputation on the 'two swords' theory and the other allegorical theories derived from Scripture by declaring that, as allegories, they cannot be used as evidence in a logical discussion. John's own proofs for the autonomy of the secular power may be as abstract as the allegorical proofs he challenges. Thus his cherished idea that the people was, under God, the source from which royal power was derived is not perhaps so certain a historical fact as he appears to think. But at all events John's approach enabled discussion to take place on a more rational level than the use of the fantasies of allegory could ever have made possible.

John applies his theory of popular sovereignty to the *Sacerdotium* as well as to the *Regnum*. Taking up the corporation theory of the decretalists, he drew from it the conclusion that the supreme authority of the Church was spread throughout all its members and not exclusively concentrated in the Papacy. The authority of the latter was derived

91

from the whole body of the faithful through election by their agents, the Cardinals. The Pope, if unworthy, could be deposed through the same medium or at a still more representative level by the General Council. John's familiarity with the rise of representative assemblies in the Europe of his time (not least in his own Dominican Order) combines with his Aristotelean outlook to make him regard monarchy tempered with aristocratic and democratic elements as the ideal form of government. Thus he desires to surround the Pope with permanent elected representatives from each province or kingdom: it is possible that he may have in mind some reform of the College of Cardinals on this basis. The General Council for him, as for an older school of canonists, may stand above the Papacy as the final ecclesiastical authority.

At first sight John may give the impression of desiring merely a return to the old conception of the Christian Commonwealth with a harmonious adjustment of relations between its two branches. But when we look closer we find that he, just as much as the opposing hierocrats, has accepted the new assumption that the *Sacerdotium* must be organized as a State on the Aristotelean definition. His difference from the papalists is that he does not, like them, rest his conception of the *Sacerdotium*'s government on an absolute monarchy. A still more fundamental difference with the hierocrats is that John does not replace the old Commonwealth with one State but with two. Each of Gelasius's complementary authorities has now become self-contained, though John still admits to each an emergency right of interference in the other's affairs. So John refrains from taking the final step of making his two authorities two separate societies.

That step was to be taken by a thinker primarily interested in repressing the ambitions of the rising national States on behalf of an ideal of rule by a universal world Empire, which he identified as that of Rome. The fact that Dante (1265–1321) was also the greatest of medieval poets is not immediately relevant to our present purpose and we can happily leave out

92

of account the labyrinthine discussions of what exactly the political references in *The Divine Comedy* mean. Dante's contribution to political thought consists largely in prose writings, particularly the *Monarchia*, all written around the period when the Emperor Henry VII (1308–1313) made his ill-fated expedition to Italy to restore the imperial power there. We know from contemporary letters of Dante that the Florentine poet-politician hailed Henry as the destined saviour of Italy from civil strife. Only a Roman Emperor could save the cradle of the Empire from chaos. It is essential to appreciate the background to the contemporary problem of the Empire in order to understand why the imperial ideal exercised such a fascination on Dante's mind.

The unity of western Europe under one secular head had never been a practical reality since Charlemagne. But the ideal of a revived Western Roman Empire had lived on under the aegis of the German monarchy and had even enjoyed a vague *de iure* primacy over the other monarchies of the west, a primacy given theoretical encouragement by the revived study of Roman law. The development of the power of the territorial monarchical states was bound to lead to a more self-conscious sense of independence on their part, a sense that would sooner or later seek for some juristic basis.

The earliest certain legal opinions in support of this national particularism come from canonist sources; Alanus, for instance, says that each king has in his own kingdom the same juridical powers as the Emperor has in the Empire. It is possible that the canonists may have been inclined to favour the legal independence of the national monarchies as a means of abasing the pretensions of the *Imperium*, the Papacy's more usual antagonist at this period. It is equally understandable that the majority of commentators on the civil law should have upheld the inalienable *de iure* supremacy of the Emperor. There was however an important stream of civilian lawyers in the middle and later thirteenth century, particularly in the kingdoms of France and Naples, who tried to apply all the

POLITICAL THOUGHT IN MEDIEVAL TIMES

prerogatives of imperial sovereignty enunciated by Roman law to their own national rulers.

It was this group of legists from which originated the celebrated formula: '*Rex est imperator in regno suo*' ('The king is Emperor in his own kingdom'), though it is still under debate which of the two centres, France or Naples, can claim priority in coining the phrase. The post-glossators (the fourteenth-century commentators on civil law) were to accept the new formula and limit the prerogatives of the Emperor to what did not amount to much more than a primacy of honour. By so doing they made it possible for Roman law to be used by the new states and so to influence the modern legal codes of western Europe.

The growing tendency to reject any pretensions of the *Imperium* to universal authority was given impetus by the Empire's almost complete collapse as an institution in the second half of the thirteenth century. By that time the German monarchy had become a permanently elective institution and the famous electoral college of seven princes, three of them ecclesiastic, had assumed the right of disposing of the succession to the monarchy at each vacancy. The Papacy had had no small share in promoting the victory of the electoral principle, doubtless out of anxiety to exclude the Hohenstauffen ambition of a strong hereditary succession. The electoral procedure as it emerged certainly showed clear traces of the influence of the methods of collegiate election laid down by canon law. During the Great Interregnum (1250–1273) in the Empire the prostration of the imperial institution was so complete that there was even talk of extinction of the imperial title and a partition of the realms attached to it on a *Realpolitik* basis by France and other interested powers. This was never actually implemented; perhaps it was felt that such a step would be too radical a break with the past. But though the danger never really materialized the very threat of it was sufficient to call forth a movement of desperate reaction from those who still clung to the imperial ideal.

Defenders of the imperial prerogatives like Jordan of Osnabruck (*c.* 1275) and Alexander of Roes (*c.* 1281) were more imperialist than the Emperors themselves when the latter were the uninspiring Hapsburgs Rudolf (1273–1291) and Albert (1298–1308). These early imperialist protagonists suffered from their inability to adduce satisfactory rational arguments for their allocation of universal political supremacy to the German monarchy. The mixture of legendary information which they provided about Charlemagne and the Trojan descent of the German race was hardly likely to be a convincing substitute.

Engelbert of Admont (*c.* 1250–1331) put forward a stronger case. He took as his starting point Aristotle's description of sufficiency, tranquillity and security as being the necessary conditions for a prosperous State and contended that these conditions could only be met by a universal Empire. Engelbert is not blind to the objections to his argument, even admitting that the universal peace his Empire seeks may never be obtained. All the same, he says, it is right for the Empire to strive towards such peace, even though it may never reach it, for it is in the very act of striving that it fulfils its eternal destiny. To a modern reader Engelbert may almost seem to anticipate Robert Louis Stevenson's 'It is better to journey than to arrive', but in fact he is rather looking back to the political pessimism of St. Augustine.

Dante was disturbed by no such doubts of the certainty of obtaining a temporal universal peace, provided the right recipe for it was followed. His own bitter experiences of Italian civic and inter-civic discord led his reflections, for which his exile gave him ample leisure, to look towards the establishment of a world monarchy as the Messianic hope of political life. Indeed Dante concluded that it was the only hope of saving mankind, collectively and individually, from those capital vices of lust, pride and covetousness which the leopard, lion and wolf so vividly symbolize in the opening canto of *The Divine Comedy*.

95

The first adumbration of Dante's theory of universal empire may be found in his unfinished treatise, the *Convivio* (probably written between 1304 and 1308). The *Convivio* might be described as a 'Teach Yourself Philosophy' course for the busy layman. It is written in vernacular Italian instead of Latin and consists of verses with an allegorical significance which is explained in each case by the author's prose commentary: if we could imagine Mr. T. S. Eliot embarking on such an enterprise we should obtain the nearest modern equivalent.

Dante treats of the *Imperium* and its functions in parenthesis to his own disagreement with what he took to be Frederick II's definition of nobility, although in fact it was Aristotle's. The definition with which Dante was quarrelling had described nobility as 'old-established wealth and good upbringing' and this did not seem to Dante to be a sufficiently ethical definition. To a modern reader it does not seem odd that Dante should venture to disagree with an Emperor of a previous period over a definition pertaining to the science of ethics; one could not easily imagine (to pursue our modern analogy) Mr. Eliot hesitating before the impropriety of challenging on a detail of Indian philosophy the opinion of Queen Victoria. What seems much odder to a modern reader is that Dante should excuse his disagreement by an elaborate analysis of the Emperor's own proper sphere. Nothing could throw into stronger relief the almost excessive respect for authority in the abstract which was characteristic of medieval thought in general and of Dante's thought in particular.

Authority itself was defined by Dante in the *Convivio* as 'something worthy of belief and obedience', the highest criterion in its own field of both theory and practice. As a convinced Aristotelean, Dante has no hesitation in awarding to the Stagirite philosopher the palm of authority in all matters pertaining to purely human reason. In the *Convivio* he described him (in terms foreshadowing *The Divine Comedy*'s phrase '*il maestro di color che sanno*') as 'the master of human

96

reason—who always first combatted the enemies of the truth and then, when he had overcome them, demonstrated the truth to them'. Aristotle is the philosphical authority *par excellence*.

For Dante this is not a merely abstract title, for philosophy is the criterion determining the correct practical behaviour of man. Dante underlines this emphasis on the practicality of philosophy by giving the first place among its branches to ethics rather than metaphysics and thus reversing the traditional scholastic classification. It was not that Dante thought that metaphysics and the life of abstract contemplation were intrinsically inferior to ethics and the life of social action; but he did think that for the majority of men they were not so immediately relevant. So it is a rather utilitarian Aristotle who is for Dante the last word in philosophical authority.

Aristotle, like any good philosopher, can only advise; he cannot compel. Indeed if he tried to compel he would be leaving the only field of authority, philosophy, in which he had any right to claim obedience. There is no evidence that Dante knew of the philosopher-kings of Plato's *Republic*; but if he had done he would have had no use for them. For him the right to use compulsive authority belongs to the political, not the philosophical hierarchy.

Dante follows the other Aristoteleans of his time in extending Aristotle's own definition of the city as the normal political unit to include the *Regnum*, but he goes a stage further by arguing that the existence of wars between *regna* demands the creation of a yet higher political authority which will pacify the whole world. Dante describes this authority by the term Monarchy and says that it will be the perfect arbitrating force; it will possess all and will therefore have no ambition to pervert its goodwill. It is thus the essential guide needed for the right development of what Dante calls *umana civilta* and which we may loosely translate as 'human civilization'. It has been suggested by Dr. Minio-Paluello and Professor d'Entrèves that the term, which is peculiar to

97

Dante may have been derived from the twelfth-century Latin translation of Aristotle's *Nicomachean Ethics*. This had used the word *civilitas* to render Aristotle's word describing the constitutional structure of a political community.

The world ruler whom Dante envisages possesses a unique authority to provide the practical guidance necessary for the peace essential for Man's civilized development. He is, to use Dante's own figure of speech, 'the rider of the human will'. This political charioteer can be none other than the Roman Empire; Dante devotes a whole chapter and a half to proving that Rome deserved world domination both by her own virtue and by divine disposition. Many of his arguments are based on a conception of historical evidence which would hardly satisfy modern standards. Dante's treatment of his authorities (in this case the Bible, Virgil and Livy) is, like that of most medieval writers, what might be described as fundamentalist: indeed his already quoted definition of what an authority is would preclude any other type of approach. But even when all due allowance has been made one cannot but regard as fantastic a technique of argument which, for example, proves the divine origin of the Roman Empire by the alleged contemporaneity of the founding of Rome and the reign of David.

The *Monarchia* seems to have been envisaged by Dante as his prose *magnum opus*; the fact that he retained sufficient interest in it to finish it, unlike the *Convivio*, bears this out. He himself tells us at the opening of its first book that he wishes to be the first writer to demonstrate the necessity of a universal monarchy. In fact only two of the main ideas of the *Monarchia* are not to be found in the preceding discussion of the Empire in the *Convivio*. But these two novelties are of paramount importance in Dante's thought.

The first is the philosophical expansion of the concept *humana civilitas*, already mentioned in the *Convivio*. Dante defines the purpose of this civilized activity as being 'always to bring into actuality the whole power of the possible intellect,

98

first for the purpose of speculation and secondly as a result and extension of this for the purpose of action'. This dark saying will be a little clearer if we think of the scholastic distinction between the soul's passive capacity to receive knowledge (the 'passive' or 'possible' intellect) and the co-ordinating power (the 'active' intellect) which made this passive capacity bring forth fruit in the form of securely grasped knowledge. The concept may well be an application to the mind of the usual medieval view of the biology of human reproduction, in which the female was thought of as occupying a necessary but purely passive role by comparison with that of the male and the planetary influences which ruled his generating powers.

No single individual, according to Dante, can ever hope to transform into actuality all the potentiality for knowledge which the passive intellect of mankind as a whole contains: he can at best acquire a fraction of the total sum of knowledge which the species is intended by its Divine Maker to attain. The species itself can only hope for success in this gigantic task if it is organized for the purpose as a co-operative unit. Only a universal community can be the midwife for the safe bringing to birth of all that man's intellect can produce.

Dante's emphasis on the unity of human intellectual activity led in his own day and later to accusations of Averroism. That religiously condemned brand of Aristotelean interpretation does indeed seem to have taught that there was only one single permanent passive intellect for the whole human race, in which individual intellects temporarily and partially shared; this idea was logically linked with Averroes's denial of the immortality of the individual soul. Did Dante actually intend, as some critics (notably Signor Bruno Nardi) assert, to teach this doctrine of the unity of the passive intellect? The evidence is not decisive enough to make a clear-cut judgement possible. Dante certainly mentions with approval Averroes's opinion on the desirability of co-operation by many individuals to actuate all mankind's intellectual

99

potentiality; but whether he takes this to mean a strict unity of man's intellect on Averroist lines is another matter. It has been contended by M. Etienne Gilson that Dante's use of the word *multitudo* proves that, far from being an Averroist, he has in mind a genuine plurality of human individual intellects engaged in a common task; such an interpretation would indeed be more in line with the profoundly individualist tone of *The Divine Comedy*, where everyone goes to hell or elsewhere very much in his own way.

It may be remarked in parenthesis that all attempts to reconstruct a so-called political Averroism from the works of Dante or any other medieval thinker have been quite unreal. The political observations of Averroes are confined to some mainly accurate but pedestrian commentaries on Plato's *Republic* and Aristotle's *Nicomachean Ethics*: in neither does Averroes attempt to propound a personal system of political philosophy. Neither from his own writings nor from those of his Latin disciples are we, in the present state of our knowledge, justified in speaking of any political Averroist scheme of thought. To try to find, as some modern writers have done, influences of such a hypothetical scheme in the statements of Dante or Marsiglio seems a rather futile speculative exercise.

The first book of the *Monarchia* is a set of variations on the theme that world monarchy is a condition for the realization of that state of peace which is essential for a fully civilized society of Mankind. The second book takes up the *Convivio's* insistence that this monarchy must be Roman and reinforces it with a profusion of not remarkably convincing arguments. The third book, however, breaks new ground by dealing with the claims of the Papacy to direct temporal authority over the Empire.

Dante treats the See of St. Peter with the utmost respect, excusing its ideological exaggerations as being due to 'zeal for the keys' and to the baneful influence of 'those who call themselves decretalists, who are ignorant of any theology and philosophy'. Although not rejecting the canonist tradition

100

altogether, Dante definitely subordinates it to the teaching of the Scriptures, the General Councils of the Church and the Fathers. Most of Dante's arguments revolve round the time-honoured allegorical and pseudo-historical cruxes of the papal-imperial debate: the sun and moon, the two swords, the Donation of Constantine and others are discussed at tiresome length. One wonders in reading these pages of the *Monarchia* how the pedantically jejune mind which seems to lie behind them could also have been the author of the poetry of the *Comedy*. Then at the very last chapter of the whole treatise the argument suddenly, if briefly, comes to life with the introduction of a startlingly original idea—that of man as having two separate destinies or 'ends'.

Previous Christian scholastic philosophy had regarded man's heavenly goal of eternal salvation as his all-sufficing end to which the subsidiary goal of temporal happiness and earthly order might be a useful aid. Dante seems to have been the first thinker to elevate the earthly destiny of Man, in particular his political and philosophical development, into an end in itself. This religiously eccentric doctrine was probably responsible for the Church's dislike of the *Monarchia*, culminating in its being placed on the Index of Prohibited Books in the sixteenth century and remaining on it until as late as 1897. But the idea of the two ends is logically bound up with the distinction already made in the *Convivio* between the spheres of the three authorities by which human behaviour should be guided.

Dante's argument is based on the assumption that, as man has a footing in both the spiritual and temporal worlds owing to his twofold material and spiritual nature, he must therefore have two ends, one for each of his two natures. The first end, symbolized by the earthly paradise, is the happiness which is obtainable in this mortal life; the other and more durable end, symbolized by the heavenly paradise, is the eternal happiness of the possession of God, obtainable only by His own assistance.

101

Each of these ends dictates the specific means to reach it. The earthly end requires obedience to pure human reason, as represented by Aristotle and operating through a principal agent, the universal Emperor; the heavenly end demands obedience to the super-rational commands of divine revelation, operating through a principal agent, the Papacy. Each of these authorities has received its commission directly from God and all will go well as long as neither makes the error of interfering in the other's appointed sphere. Dante in short extends the principle of the autonomy of the State, already partially admitted by Christian Aristoteleans like St. Thomas, to an absolute degree. It may be true, as a plausible suggestion of M. Gilson has it, that Dante was influenced in formulating his theory by the statement in St. Thomas's commentary on Aristotle's *Nicomachean Ethics* that 'the Philosopher' regarded politics as the 'consideration of the final end of human life'.

Dante certainly goes further than anyone before him in breaking with the old ideal of a unified Christian Commonwealth controlled in both its branches by a revealed tradition of thought and action. Instead he tries to substitute a carefully balanced and complete dualism, in which State and Church are quite independent of each other, though necessarily co-operative. There is no question of a lay State, for the State's end is just as much subject to Divine Providence as is that of the Church. There may even be something to be said for the recent view of Professor d'Entrèves that Dante looks on the Empire in an Augustinian manner as a bridle for the sin which had perverted the naturally good political community. This would bring Dante closer to the earlier medieval position but would not affect the fact that his ultimate political unit of thought is no longer Christendom but a world State. It is true that he implies that such a State would be Christian, but the logic of his own insistence on rational philosophy as the State's essential foundation would lead to the conclusion that Christianity was not indispensable to the State as such. Dante

102

himself does not face this difficulty in his theory unless, as Professor d'Entrèves contends, *The Divine Comedy* marks a repudiation of the doctrine of the two ends. It was left to another Italian thinker to press to their ultimate extreme the claims for the new autonomy of the State.

‡‡‡‡‡‡‡‡‡‡‡‡‡‡‡‡‡‡‡‡‡‡‡‡‡‡‡‡‡‡‡‡‡‡‡

CHAPTER VII

THE STATE COMES OF AGE

T HE details of the life of Marsiglio of Padua (*c.* 1280–*c.* 1343) are scanty and uncertain. Like Dante, he came from an Italian city republic which had been periodically on bad terms with the clerical estate because of that estate's claim to judicial immunity. In the 1280s Padua had passed stringent laws virtually outlawing its clergy and had only knuckled under after interdict and excommunication by the Papacy. Marsiglio saw this papal interference writ even larger when as a man in his thirties he took part in the confused struggles between papalists and imperialists in northern Italy in the decade following Henry VII's expedition. Interspersed with this political activity were periods of study at the Universities of Padua and Paris. Marsiglio seems to have been the first of medieval writers on politics to have had a primarily medical training; medical expressions and analogies figure considerably in his writings.

The book which was to make him famous, the *Defensor Pacis*, was finished in 1324 after some years of residence in Paris. The identity of its author was not suspected until two years later when Marsiglio judged it best to leave Paris hurriedly in the company of John of Jandun, a famous Averroist philosopher. The association of the two men has led to modern suggestions that John was part-author of the *Defensor*. But a recent investigation of John's own undisputed works (which include remarks on politics) by Professor A. Gewirth shows that John held views on government which emphasized its ethical function in the usual medieval scholastic manner, and that these views are quite remote from those expressed in the *Defensor*.

The two fugitives made their way to the court of Louis of

104

Bavaria (1314–1346), now claiming the imperial title in the teeth of Pope John XXII (1316–1334), who still attempted to vindicate the outdated papal ambition to supervise and confirm imperial elections. Marsiglio joined Louis's fantastic Italian expedition of 1327, when Louis was crowned in Rome by an alleged representative of the *populus Romanus* and an Antipope of his own creation was set up. But the charade ended in retreat and John XXII, thundering implacable condemnations from Avignon, was never seriously threatened. Marsiglio spent the rest of his life under Louis's protection, writing several minor treatises in his capacity as imperial apologist. The first indication of his death is given in 1343 in an address by Pope Clement VI (1342–1352), who refers to him as already deceased and remarks that the *Defensor Pacis* was the most heretical work which he had ever read.

Marsiglio's system was certainly *sui generis* but it is also true that his results were obtained by reinterpretation of traditionally recognized authorities. His chief source apart from the Scriptures was Aristotle; but Marsiglio's Aristotle was the empirical scientist rather than the metaphysician. Aristotle's concept of the final cause of politics (the good life) is largely left out of account and instead the discussion turns on the efficient cause (the actual technique whereby government may function in the smoothest possible way). Marsiglio is willing to quote from canonists and theologians when they can be pressed into the service of his argument. He had had no systematic training in either canon law or theology but his range of quotation is for an amateur impressive, even if he obtained it from ready-made source collections. His acquaintance with civil law seems rather less, though some scholars have seen in Roman law the inspiration for his theory of popular sovereignty. It is likely however that for the latter we need look no further than his own practical experience of the contemporary Italian city State, with its offices and committees controllable, at any rate in theory, by the general body of citizens. It is from a certain type of Italian republicanism

105

that Marsiglio inherited his anti-clerical and anti-papal outlook. The Lombard towns, allies of the Papacy in the eleventh
and twelfth centuries, now saw the most pressing threats to
their autonomy in papal claims to direct political power and
papal military interventions in northern Italy. Dante's civic
experiences had made him equally critical of papal politics in
Italy; but while the Florentine poet had turned for a remedy
to a universal secular monarch Marsiglio was content to urge
the claims of the separate States of his time to exclusive control
of their own affairs.

It is a tribute to the hard-hitting vitality of the *Defensor
Pacis* that it should have aroused such a storm of controversy
in modern study and interpretation of it. Most critics under-
standably find it hard to be perfectly non-partisan when faced
with the themes treated by Marsiglio. At the same time it is
regrettable that so many writers on Marsilian thought have
all too often taken the opportunity to interpret it in the dubious
light of their own convictions for or against the Catholic
Church, the lay State, democracy, liberalism, totalitarianism
and whatever not. The result has been that the study of
Marsiglio has suffered from being put into anachronistic
terms of reference. We need to discover not what the *Defensor
Pacis* means for the twentieth century but what it meant for
the fourteenth.

The avowed intention of the whole treatise is to isolate the
causes of order and tranquillity within the State (a word
which Marsiglio himself never uses but which exactly ex-
presses his own various paraphrastic terms defining his ideal of
political self-sufficiency). Dictio I, the first section of the work,
deals with this problem in general terms applicable, as the
author believes, to any period in history or to any race.
Dictio II contends that this *sine qua non* of political stability
is threatened by the *Sacerdotium's* claim to a separate legal
system with its own coercive powers. It is this intrusion into
temporal affairs by the Papacy and its hierarchy, declares
Marsiglio, which is responsible for a dangerous division of

106

authority in Christian States. Dictio II also contains the practical programme for bringing to an end this disastrous state of affairs and it was probably to serve as a frame for this provocative anti-clerical manifesto that the whole treatise was produced.

It is a mistake, however, to dismiss Dictio I as a mere formal preparation for the more important polemical campaign of Dictio II. The first Dictio contains indispensable material defining the science of politics as Marsiglio saw it. The starting point is an assertion of the necessity of peace for the political community. Marsiglio's conception of peace draws some of its supporting quotations from the song of the angels at Bethlehem and the Scriptural words of Jesus. Nevertheless it is in essence a plain *bourgeois* desire for sufficient material tranquillity to permit the smooth interchange of economic and social benefits. This prepares the reader for what is to be the distinguishing feature of Marsilian political thought—a down-to-earth concentration on political life dictated by the material human conditions of economics, biology and psychology.

Marsiglio might with justice be described as the first political sociologist of the Middle Ages. At the same time he is not untrue to Aristotle when he develops the theme of the political community as an organism composed of proportionately differentiated parts; Marsiglio's medical background leads him to put this in terms of analogy to the rightly-proportioned members of the healthy animal body. 'Tranquillity,' he tells us, 'would be the good ordering of a city or kingdom by which any one of its parts would be able to carry out fully the activities which befit it according to reason and to the purposes for which it was instituted.' It will be noticed that Marsiglio, like other medieval Aristoteleans, takes it for granted that Aristotle's political unit of the city may legitimately be extended to include the *Regnum*, and the attempt to combine Marsiglio's Italian background of the city with the larger Western unit of the territorial kingdom, forms an interesting and recurrent theme of the whole book.

107

The *Defensor* rapidly sketches the development of human society, closely following Aristotle's scheme of evolution from family *via* village to city. There is nothing new here apart from the Old Testament analogies brought in to illustrate the alleged development. This is the first of many occasions on which the Old Testament is appealed to by Marsiglio in confirmation or illustration of his arguments. This frequent use of Old Testament sources would seem to invalidate a modern interpretation of Marsiglio by M. de Lagarde, which represents him as following the Waldensians and other medieval heretics in not accepting the Old Testament as valid Scripture. It is true that he says that a large number of its provisions no longer bind Christians; but exactly the same point was made by St. Paul.

Marsiglio traces in this development from family to State a growing specialization and differentiation of activities, all paving the way to a common end, the acquisition of those things necessary 'for life and even the good life'. Here Marsiglio shows that he is well aware of the teleological orientation of Aristotle's political thought. His point of separation from Aristotle was paradoxically due to the Christian background of his age. Marsiglio understands 'the good life' in two senses, one in relation to this world, the other in relation to the eternal world. Unlike Aristotle, he cannot entertain the view that the State can provide for both these fundamental desires of Man; on the other hand he wishes to vindicate for the lay power its own autonomous sphere against clerical hierocracy. He does not want to banish religion or laicize the State; on the contrary, he asserts the complementary need for both political ruler and religious leaders. He is, however, emphatic that the two spheres of the good life must not be confused and it is this anxiety which leads him to treat the science of human political government in isolation from religious obligations and truths which, he says in Averroist fashion, cannot in any case be discussed in terms derived from human rational categories.

In his assessment of the human psychological factors which help or hinder correct political development Marsiglio strikes a balance between the extremes of pessimism and optimism. He takes the hopeful view that men by nature seek what he describes as 'the sufficient life'; this would seem to be equivalent to what he described as a drive towards self-fulfilment in a healthy sense. Any men who do not desire this must be, Marsiglio assumes, 'deformed', incapacitated from being truly human. Here again Marsiglio seems to have the analogy of medical health, physical or mental, in mind.

This faith in ordinary human nature is balanced by a realization that its unrestricted expression would be bound to lead to anarchy. Marsiglio makes no mention of Original Sin, in accordance with his intention of explaining politics in purely human terms. Instead he explains conflicts between men as due to the clash of contrary 'elements' present in every individual and which give rise to the passions and emotions; Marsiglio here transforms an accepted medieval medical doctrine into a diagnosis of individual and collective psychology. He concludes that these 'elements' can only be harmonized by the co-ordinative control of a clearly articulated social life. The raw material of human nature must be brought into tractable shape by the art of politics.

The principles of this art are strictly practical. Marsiglio distinguishes between 'immanent' and 'transient' acts. The distinction, which seems to be all his own, may be paraphrased as referring to the world of interior thought and the world of exterior action respectively. It is only with the second, Marsiglio declares, that social life *per se* is concerned; the purely interior life of a man is a matter for his conscience and his religion, whose sanctions are not of this world. Marsiglio admits however in almost Machiavellian fashion that the moral dictates of religion, with their threats of supernatural penalties for disobedience, may be useful adjuncts to political authority in its task of preserving discipline.

After enumerating the different classes of the community

in Aristotelean fashion and emphasizing that the sacerdotal class's purpose in society can only be assumed on a basis of faith, not proved by reason, Marsiglio comes to what he regards as the directing force in society. He describes this as the 'human legislator' (*legislator humanus*), a peculiarly Marsilian term. Marsiglio apparently understands by it the political community as a whole, the ultimate sovereign authority. This *legislator humanus* assigns to each class its specific duties within the State and distributes individuals to each class according to their aptitudes.

The class with which Marsiglio is particularly concerned is what he terms 'the ruling section' (*pars principans*), the portion of the State which carries out the duties of executive government. He falls back on Aristotle once more to define the various forms which the *pars principans* may take. He himself prefers a republican form of elective government or at least an elective monarchy. Later in Dictio I various arguments for and against hereditary monarchy are listed and Marsiglio reaches the conclusion that better government may be expected from a *régime* whose authority is periodically subject to re-institution by the ultimate sovereign, the *legislator humanus*. Years of residence in France, the hereditary monarchy *par excellence*, had apparently done nothing to modify Marsiglio's adherence to the Italian republican tradition. May his expression of preference even have had something to do with the readiness of the French government to collaborate in the Church's condemnation of Marsiglio?

Whatever form government may take, its primary purpose is to promulgate and enforce the law. But what is law? Marsiglio uses the word *lex* throughout his definitions in Dictio I, though it might be argued that the first meaning he treats ('a natural inclination of the senses to any action or passion') is more in keeping with one of St. Thomas's categories of *ius*. Other meanings of *lex* mentioned by Marsiglio include patterns elaborated by mental processes and the admonitions of religion. But Marsiglio contends that none of

110

them can be equated with the truly political definition of law, for they all lack coercive power. He declares that it is this capacity to enforce decisions by material means of pressure which differentiates the law which the earthly political community administers from any other form of law. No moral precept can be called a law unless it is embodied in a coercive enactment from the appropriate political authority, the *pars principans*.

A great deal has sometimes been made of the assertion that Marsiglio bases his philosophy of law on force and coercion instead of conformity to a moral code as, for example, does St. Thomas. Yet Aquinas himself, as we have seen, defines the power of compulsion as one of the essential characteristics of law. Nor is it true to say that Marsiglio disregards the moral factor in lawmaking. He follows up his definition of law as coercive with the statement that a knowledge of the principles of morality is essential if a law is to be 'perfect'. As an illustration of a defective law he cites the Germanic custom of the *wergild*, which enabled punishment for murder to be commuted for a monetary fine. Marsiglio remarks that even though this law had the necessary coercive force behind it, yet it was lacking in an essential constituent of true law, i.e. 'a legitimate and true enactment of things which are just'.

We may reasonably ask whether Marsiglio's position, as thus defined by himself, is very different from that of St. Thomas. Marsiglio places most of his emphasis on the element of will in law, St. Thomas places most of his on the element of reason. But to say that Marsiglio's conception of law is purely voluntarist would be as false as to say that St. Thomas's conception was entirely rationalist. Marsiglio's legal philosophy may be couched in his own terminology but it does not constitute a radical departure from medieval precedent.

The rule of the law, declares Marsiglio, is preferable to that of any one man, however good. The reason for this is the fact that the law embodies the collective wisdom and experience of the whole community; Marsiglio puts this idea in a

111

vivid phrase: 'The law is an eye made up of many eyes'. We may suspect that Marsiglio is here not only following Aristotle in arguing against absolute monarchy as such; he may also have in mind a stock hierocratic argument that the Pope, as the earthly head of Christianity, had the right to rule over and above the positive law of both *Regnum* and *Sacerdotium*.

The twelfth chapter of Dictio I explains the ideal mechanics of lawmaking as Marsiglio sees them. The terms of a law itself may well be drafted by the more legally and morally expert members of the community, but until their recommendations are given coercive validity by the community as a whole they cannot be considered as law in a political sense. They remain law in the sense of non-coercive precepts. The proper efficient cause of law is therefore, according to Marsiglio, 'the people or whole body of citizens or its weightier part, through its choice or wish expressed in a definite form of wording in the general assembly of citizens'. Marsiglio almost immediately defines this 'weightier part' (*valentior pars*) as being conditioned by 'the quantity and quality of the persons in the community for which the law is to be made'.

Until the present century the phrase referring to the 'quality' of citizens was not known to students of the *Defensor Pacis*, as it had been omitted from the first and subsequent printed editions of the book. It was therefore tempting to see in Marsiglio's definition a clear anticipation of majoritarian democratic rule. This view, so congenial to nineteenth-century liberal commentators, was shown to be false during the present century by C. W. Previté-Orton, who in the course of preparing his critical edition of the *Defensor*, found the additional phrase '*in qualitate*' to be present in most of the manuscripts he examined. Previté-Orton's discovery led to a perhaps too extreme reaction against the liberal view of Marsiglio, who was now depicted on the evidence of the two telltale words as an advocate of oligarchy and perhaps even a disguised totalitarianism. The recent full-scale treatment in English by A. Gewirth argues convincingly against such

112

exaggerations by pointing out that Marsiglio does in fact link up the *valentior pars* with his previous assertion of a desire for the communal and individual good among all but the deformed. It is only the latter who are likely through their perverse nature to upset the unanimity of community decisions. Marsiglio plainly regards the *valentior pars* as composing the vast majority of the community—the normal undeformed citizens. In their persons the claims of both quality and quantity are reconciled.

Despite resemblances to principles of canon and civil law on collegiate voting it does seem that Marsiglio is here breaking new ground. Previous medieval thought had tended to hand over the care of the common good to a relatively small circle of persons or even to one person alone. Marsiglio insists that although the 'discovery' and framing of laws was the prerogative of the *pars principans* and its experts, the ordinary free citizen is perfectly competent to form and express a judgement on the usefulness or otherwise of the proposed laws. Marsiglio justifies this by an analogy with the arts and crafts such as painting and architecture. Only a minority of human beings actually have the gift of original creation and design; but the non-creative majority is not thereby debarred from judging the finished work. Politics is an art in which the government is the artist while the citizens form the body of critics, both being equally necessary to a healthy political life.

Marsiglio gives other reasons for his view. One is the commonsense argument that a community is more likely to obey laws to which it has given its own approval. Authority as well as reason is called in support by a reference to Aristotle's conception of a 'polity' or mixed State in his *Politics*; Marsiglio explicitly claims that his own *pars valentior* conforms to the Aristotelean requirements. As he was ignorant of Greek, Marsiglio was unaware that he was falsifying Aristotle's true meaning which aimed at balancing the majority principle in voting with a preference for those voters possessing greater

113

property. Marsiglio contrasts his own republican democracy with what he declares to be the oligarchic tendencies of the Church lawyers of his period and his theory of popular sovereignty does in fact form the basis of his attack on the *Sacerdotium*'s claim to temporal power.

Most of the last chapters of Dictio I are devoted to a discussion of the powers and duties of the *pars principans*. Marsiglio compares this function of the State to the heart in the human body; each directs and preserves the organism to which it is attached. So there can no more be two governing sections in the State than there can be two hearts in the human body. Beside this basic requirement the actual nature of the *pars principans* is of secondary importance. It may be either hereditary or elective monarchy or (as Marsiglio seems to prefer) a board which has moral if not numerical unity. The essential is that the power of the *pars principans*, after it has been conferred by the *legislator humanus*, cannot and must not be shared with any other authority; otherwise division and ultimate anarchy will confront the State.

Marsiglio has sometimes been accused of nullifying his surface democracy by the absolute power with which his *legislator humanus* invests his *pars principans*. The accusation would be just only if it could be shown that Marsiglio, like one school of civilian lawyers, regarded the transfer of authority from people to prince as irrevocable. Examination of Marsiglio's argument makes clear that authority is not wholly transferred; the *legislator humanus* retains ultimate sovereignty and can check, even depose, the *pars principans* when necessary. Marsiglio, like St. Thomas, does not advocate punishment of the *pars principans* for minor abuses as this might, by bringing government into disrepute, do more harm than good. Once again the practice of the thirteenth-century Italian city State seems to be at the back of Marsiglio's mind.

Dictio II brings us to the long-prepared assault on the political claims of the contemporary Church. The primary interest of this is perhaps rather for the theologian or ecclesiastical historian than for the student of political thought, so it will not be examined here in as much detail as Dictio I has been. Marsiglio's revolutionary suggestions for reorganizing the Church and destroying the *Sacerdotium* as a governmental force depend ultimately on his doctrines of popular sovereignty and representation as presented in Dictio I. His denial of inherent coercive validity to spiritual precepts, unless they be formally promulgated as laws by the State, destroys at a stroke the claims to independence and even supremacy made by the legal system of the *Sacerdotium*.

He defines the Church as 'the whole body of the faithful who believe in and invoke the name of Christ'. In itself this was not necessarily an unorthodox definition; we have already met with something like it in the writings of the twelfth-century decretists, particularly Huguccio, who had interpreted the meaning of the term 'the Roman Church' as being 'the whole body of the faithful'. The expression 'the congregation of the faithful' had come to be accepted as the primary definition of the Church by many canonists of the fourteenth century, though naturally without thought of drawing any anti-hierarchical conclusions from it. The drawing of such conclusions marked the real novelty of Marsiglio's theory of the Church.

For him the 'whole body of the faithful' (which is in effect the *legislator humanus* at prayer) must be through the *pars principans* the governing authority in the religious as well as in the political community. It alone had the right to control clerical appointments, to impose discipline on individual members of the Church, even to excommunicate. The sacerdotal hierarchy had not been given any coercive jurisdiction by Christ, even in spiritual matters. The hierarchical leadership of Papacy and episcopate is nothing more than a man-made device. The Papacy in particular can claim nothing but a traditional primacy of honour among its fellow-bishops. Marsiglio, like John of Paris, rejects the allegorical interpretation of Scriptural texts on which the hierocratic arguments

115

were often based, but he goes much further than John by casting doubt on the Petrine basis for the Papal claims to spiritual government. It is this section of the *Defensor* which orthodox Catholicism would have reason to brand as heretical.

It is not Marsiglio's intention to advocate a State without religion. Nor in fact does he question the traditional medieval assumption that the secular power is bound to uphold orthodoxy. In some ways he even takes to extremes the traditional concept by maintaining that the secular power alone may use coercive strength to enforce obedience to religious truth. But how is this truth to be decided, granted the Marsilian contention that the Papacy possesses no finally unchallengeable power to define doctrine?

Marsiglio finds a way out by appealing to the infallibility of a rightly constituted General Council; in this appeal he was again following in canonistic footsteps—but the Council as envisaged by him was a Council with a difference. It was to be summoned by the secular power in the person of a vague authority called by Marsiglio 'the faithful human legislator with no superior'. Marsiglio may here be making a genuflection to the ideal of a Christian universal empire of the type envisaged by Dante, though he shows remarkable lack of enthusiasm for a world monarchy on the few occasions when he explicitly refers to it. In fact he is far from certain of the desirability of universal international peace, remarking cynically that war is one of Nature's ways to reduce the world's surplus population. It is also possible that 'the faithful human legislator with no superior' may be the Holy Roman Emperor, Marsiglio's protector, or it may even be any suzerain feudal overlord.

Once summoned, the Council is to be elected by the faithful in the various Christian political communities in much the same way as laws are approved by the *legislator humanus* in political affairs, i.e. by the judgement of 'the weightier part'. Laymen as well as clerics are to be eligible for election as representatives to the Council—another notable break with

116

canonical tradition. The decisions of such a Council are infallible but need the co-operation of the *legislator humanus* in each State before they can be enforced. Marsiglio does not tackle the obvious difficulty in his system: what happens if the various independent 'legislators' of different States disagree about confirmation or enforcement of Conciliar decisions? How is the complete control of the Church in each State by the *legislator humanus* to be reconciled with the infallibility of the universal Church which Marsiglio still seeks to preserve? Marsiglio does not attempt to deal with the problem of a clash between these hardly consistent elements in his system.

We do not claim to have listed here all of the 240 unorthodox statements which Pope Clement VI found in the *Defensor Pacis*, but perhaps enough has been said to make clear that here was a real challenge, not only to the *Sacerdotium*'s claims to temporal supremacy but even to its own spiritual autonomy. With Marsiglio the *Regnum* of ,earlier Christian times has frankly become the State, finding its natural origin in the desires and wills of men as they actually are and no longer ashamed of itself as a *pis aller* due to the Fall.

The democratic system of representation advocated by Marsiglio is in complete consistency with the new position. If the criterion of political power is to be the will of a majority of normal human beings, then a system of elective representation is the most likely to give accurate expression to their wishes. Republicanism is an essential part of Marsiglio's system; but this is not to say that the system could not be used, after its republicanism had been abstracted, for the benefit of absolutism. The *Defensor*'s first English translator, William Marshall (1535), was to treat the book to such a surgical operation to make it fit for use as a propaganda weapon by Henry VIII (1509–1547).

And yet Marsiglio's novelty and modernity must not be over-emphasized. We have noticed a number of ways in which he is conditioned by the ideas and terminology of the older medieval world. Most striking of all is his attempt to preserve

117

the close connection of Christianity with the political order, when the logic of his own division between religion and politics would seem to demand a separation; we noted that it is in this matter that his theory runs into most difficulties. If Dictio II is the focus of the whole treatise it is also its weakest sector. Marsiglio did not, perhaps could not, think of solving this logical difficulty by frankly dissolving the connection of the Christian Church with the State. Yet his transfer of final power in both *Sacerdotium* and *Regnum* to the sovereign people foreshadows the end of the distinctive political role which Western Europe had conceded to the Church in varying degrees since the conversion of Constantine. Though even Marsiglio did not realize it, the Christian Commonwealth, in the form in which the Middle Ages had created it, was ceasing to exist and in its place a new political *leitmotiv* was coming into control—the modern State.

CHAPTER VIII

THE AGE OF AMBIGUITY

No PERIOD in European history is more difficult to assess or interpret than the two hundred years between Marsiglio of Padua and Martin Luther. It is not that evidence on which to base a judgement is lacking or fragmentary; the difficulty lies in how we are to interpret the mass of evidence which we already have. The controversy on where to place the respective chronological limits of the Middle Ages and the Renaissance is the most obvious illustration of the problem which confronts the historian of every branch of human activity, from art to economics, during these centuries. Perhaps the most reasonable solution is that which regards the change in the period as one of emphasis rather than of revolutionary transformation; but even this way out still leaves in dispute what elements in their classical and medieval heritage these centuries tended to emphasize and what they tended to undervalue.

The student of political thought is not exempt from these problems. This may explain why there have been such wide divergencies of opinion and approach among modern writers in estimating the general trends of fourteenth- and fifteenth-century political thought and in interpreting the standpoints of individual thinkers. Some may regard the period as chiefly characterized by the steady growth of absolutist systems of government in Church and State; others may point to the continued and even intensified vitality of representative institutions. Some again may cite the gradually dissolving connection between secular and spiritual powers as a prelude to the de-Christianization of European thought on politics; others may argue that it was reserved for these centuries to make the most ambitious attempt to organize Christendom

119

through the Conciliar movement into a corporately articulate society. Such differences of modern emphasis are but a reflection of the tension running through the period itself, a tension which was disquietingly felt in its own keenest intellects. These centuries had begun to criticize and even to destroy their medieval past but they still cherished its traditions and dreamed of renovating them on more solid foundations. It is this ambiguity in the period which perhaps constitutes its chief fascination.

The whole period may be treated for convenience in terms of three main tensions which run through the stream of its thought. These may be defined respectively as: firstly, the opposition between the continued belief in an objective natural law as the basis for political life, and tendencies which challenged this assumption: secondly, the continued debate on the distribution of authority between ruler and community, complicated by the deductions drawn from representative practices: and thirdly, the gradual disintegration of the medieval conception of a Christian Commonwealth despite various attempts to revivify it.

In theory the obligations and rights stemming from natural law continued to be the underlying foundation of political society. At the very end of the period St. Thomas More constructed in his *Utopia* (1516) a picture of an ideal society based on the premises of natural law and natural religion without the benefit of the light of revelation. The apparent incompatibility of More's naturalism and apparent deism in the *Utopia* with his final martyrdom in defence of papal ecclesiastical government disappears when we place him in the context of the distinction between the spheres of reason and revelation which the revival of Aristotle had taught to the later Middle Ages. More places his ideally natural State in stark contrast to the land-grabbing and politically dishonest England of his own time and draws the unspoken moral.

An earlier English writer on politics, Sir John Fortescue (*c.* 1394–*c.* 1476), in his treatises *De Natura Legis Naturae*

120

and *De Laudibus Legum Angliae*, is equally insistent on the necessity of the natural law as the basis of the positive law of a particular political community. Fortescue, like More, was a lawyer by training and profession but he was, also like More, well read in theology and his arguments provide an interesting blend of the two disciplines, conditioned by the circumstances of the contemporary English scene. In the *De Natura Legis Naturae* we find Fortescue upholding the claims of the Lancastrian dynasty in the Wars of the Roses on the ground of their conformity to the precepts of natural law which, says this anti-feminist Chief Justice, debars succession through the female line (as claimed by the Yorkists).

In Nicholas of Cusa (*c.* 1400–1464), most learned of fifteenth-century Churchmen, we find the natural law basis of the State expressed in more systematically philosophical terms. In his *De concordantia Catholica*, a blueprint for the reform of both Church and State on a basis of harmonious co-operation between the rulers and ruled in each, Nicholas contends that 'every legal ordinance is rooted in natural law'; otherwise it is not valid. He then takes up the Stoic and Patristic tradition of the original equality of all men who, he says, 'by nature are all free'. We shall discuss later the deductions about political authority which Nicholas drew from this axiom; for the moment let us only notice that here again we meet the assumption that a fundamental natural law is the sustaining power for political realities.

Such was indeed the predominant tradition of the age we are discussing; but a more sceptical current of thought was not lacking. We have already noticed Marsiglio's biologizing of the natural law concept. His contemporary and fellow refugee from the Papacy, the English Franciscan William of Ockham (*c.* 1290–1349), does not question the validity of natural law, but makes a significant change of emphasis in describing its source. He sees its origin not in the immutable categories of the Divine Reason but in the arbitrary will of God. This theory is in accordance with the generally voluntarist trend of

121

Ockham's theology and ethics. For him all law must be based on the will of some competent authority.

In his *Breviloquium*, written in protest against the excesses of papal *plenitudo potestatis* in both *Regnum* and *Sacerdotium*, Ockham argues that judgement on the title-deeds of papal temporal power is best carried out, not by theologians but by experts in Civil Law. If any impingement on the sphere of natural law occurs, the principal deciding authority must be Holy Scripture, which Ockham ranks above canonistic pronouncements as the Church's ideal *vade-mecum*. Ockham here seems to be returning to the older medieval conflation (as in Gratian) between divine and natural law, but in practice his influence could not fail to weaken the connection between pure reason and natural law which the thirteenth-century Aristoteleans had been at such pains to establish.

The same reliance on revelation rather than reason is evident in his vindication of the rights of the Christian community against the Papacy on the basis of what Ockham describes as 'the evangelical law of liberty' instead of on an abstract system of natural rights. Two hundred years later Luther (1483–1546), working on an even sharper separation between reason and faith, founded his 'liberty of a Christian man' on individual possession of justifying grace and abolished rational natural law from his scheme of thought as firmly as he had abolished natural religion from his theology.

Nearer to Ockham's own day his fellow-Oxonian John Wycliffe (*c.* 1320–1384) reached an equally extreme standpoint in his rejection of a purely natural basis for political power. Ockham's position had been carefully nuanced with qualifications preventing a complete divorce from the rationalist attitude to the subject of natural law; but Wycliffe rejects the rationalist position completely. He performs the *volte-face* of taking over the theory of *dominium* as based on grace, which had come to him via Richard Fitzralph (*d.* 1360), Archbishop of Armagh, from Giles of Rome and other Augustinians, and applying it to the *Sacerdotium*. The validity of the

122

jurisdiction of any member of the sacerdotal hierarchy now depended on his freedom from mortal sin. Wycliffe's ultimate rejection of the sacramental principle in favour of a proto-Protestant religious individualism based on predestination accounts for the ferocity with which his followers were persecuted by the orthodox.[1]

His view of secular authority was more favourable. The monarch's power was instituted by God as a remedy for sin, and it therefore possesses a divine sanction which does not desert it even when monarchy is unjust; Wycliffe regards resistance to a secular ruler as in all circumstances unlawful. Here as with Ockham the medieval ideal of government as based on a rational natural law is undermined; instead political authority is linked to an arbitrary divine command. But despite such challenging voices the traditional connection of authority with the law of reason was preserved and was to continue as a strong force in thought on politics into modern times.

The second in our triad of tensions takes us to the concrete practical issue of the ruler's relation to the positive law of his community. The upholding of the traditional laws and customs of a community and the protection of individual and corporate rights within it were still conceived as the main tasks of government. All were in agreement that in ordinary circumstances the monarch was to be allowed a wide degree of freedom in deciding how he could best carry out his duties to the realm. The absolutist elements in Roman law, expressed in such phrases as 'the prince is not subject to the law' ('*princeps legibus solutus*'), perhaps encouraged a tendency to exalt the sovereign will of the monarch at the expense of the idea of his obligations to the people and the law. It has indeed been

[1] The relationship between the Wycliffite doctrines and the Hussite movement in Bohemia is a thorny problem which has been much discussed. The views on politics of the various branches of the Hussites themselves form an interesting chapter of political thought and practice but have been omitted here as perhaps peripheral in relation to the main streams of medieval thought.

argued that the fourteenth- and fifteenth-century Civilian lawyers were the pioneer architects of the theory of the Divine Right of Kings.

There may be some truth in this, but it has also been pointed out that most medieval rulers used these arguments from Roman law largely to justify their own power to dispense in unusual circumstances from the letter of the common law. The levying of extraordinary taxation in a time of national emergency was the most frequent case in point and in such cases the Aristotelean principle of equity was also frequently appealed to. It would seem therefore that the absolutism inherent in Roman law was not incompatible in practice with the Germanic tradition of customary law which continued to be the main element in medieval secular government.

We have seen how one of the features of the Germanic tradition had been the monarch's duty to seek the advice of the community through its chief men and how this conception was given clearer outline through its association with the Roman and canonical concept of representation. The thirteenth-century representative assemblies were still called into existence very much at the discretion of the monarchy in the large territorial states of the west; only in smaller city units such as those which inspired the *Defensor Pacis* was it possible to look on representation as a permanently essential part of legislative government. Yet the fourteenth and fifteenth centuries were to see movements in the same direction even in the territorial kingdoms. England is of course the most striking example. During the fourteenth century Parliament became the accepted means of formulating national grievances and of solemnly declaring and promulgating the law; at the end of the century it was even used to register the deposition of an allegedly unworthy monarch, Richard II (1377–1399).

It is going too far to think of Parliament as holding the same sovereign and legislative power which it was to obtain in the seventeenth and later centuries. As yet it was still rather a collaboration of monarchy and community to secure for each their due rights under the law. In the middle of the fifteenth century Fortescue can define this collaboration as making up a constitution which is 'regal and political', the word 'political' being used in the Aristotelean sense of a 'mixed' constitution; Fortescue explicitly acknowledges his debt for the phrase to St. Thomas's *De Regimine Principum*. Sir John deliberately contrasts the English *régime* with that obtaining in France, which he regards with patriotic disdain as a purely despotic government. Yet the States-General of France and the Cortes of the Spanish kingdoms were still far from moribund in the later Middle Ages and were often capable of energetic action in defence of their prerogatives. The true reason for their future eclipse by comparison with their English counterpart is probably the paradoxical one that their monarchies were not able to associate them with their centralizing schemes to the same degree as was possible in England; the continental estates tended to remain provincial rather than national in their outlook and paid the penalty.

The possibility of friction between the monarchical and representative principles was still largely a matter for the future as far as the secular states were concerned; but during our period a full-scale conflict between them had taken place in the internal government of the *Sacerdotium*. This conflict was the result of the situation arising from a disputed election to the Papacy in 1378, which led to the so-called Great Schism in the Western Church (1378–1417). The long division between rival papal obediences had revealed the breakdown of the traditional system of Church government, based on the monarchical concentration of all powers in the hands of the Pope. Now the papal centralizing force was gravely weakened and even discredited by the perpetuation of the schism and other solutions for the problem of the distribution of authority within the *Sacerdotium* began to come to the fore.

We have already noticed how the canonistic tradition of the thirteenth century had moved towards regarding the Church as a corporate body in the legal sense of this term. The

fourteenth-century canonists continued and developed this line
of thought but do not seem to have perceived that its logical
conclusion was that the Papacy, as representative head of the
ecclesiastical corporation, must therefore be derivative from
the whole body of the Church. The canonists of the pre-
schism period still asserted a strict papalist theory of *plenitudo
potestatis* but did not attempt any synthesis with the 'corporation theory' which they applied to the Church in ever-
increasing measure. It needed only the more enkindling concept of the Church as the 'mystical Body of Christ', a New
Testament and Patristic doctrine, to make the corporation
theory the ally of a theory of a representative General Council
as the highest Church authority.

The relationship of Council to Papacy had, of course,
been a topic of debate by both decretists and decretalists, but
it was during the fourteenth century that various anti-papal
publicists began to appeal to the Conciliar principle as a curb
on what they regarded as the excesses of papal authority. Even
so no widespread theory of Conciliar supremacy over the Pope
emerged before the crisis of the Great Schism. Marsiglio, whose
extreme Conciliarism we have already examined, was a voice
crying in the wilderness; a feature of the Conciliar apologists
of the 'classic' period of Constance (1414–1418) and Basle
(1431–1449) is their denunciation of Marsiglio's ideas. William
of Ockham is often cited as an advocate of Conciliar supremacy
but a closer examination of the confusing network of argument
and counter-argument in his massive *Dialogus* reveals that,
if anything, he was a critic of the Conciliar principle. The
individualist presuppositions of his nominalist philosophy
prevented him from granting to any representative body
more than a fictitious personality and in any case, as he
explicitly says, he cannot see why a number of separately
fallible persons should when collected together have any
greater claim to infallibility than the Pope. As far as we can
determine from this bafflingly obscure writer, Ockham was
prepared to entertain extreme scepticism on the infallibility

of all the established Church authorities; he echoes with complacency the more startling decretist speculations about the possible preservation of orthodoxy by one person alone, even a woman or a baptized infant.

The Conciliar thinkers of the early fifteenth century were far more anxious than either Marsiglio or Ockham to preserve intact the traditional hierarchical fabric. They were all strict believers in clerical monopoly of Church government and had no sympathy with Marsilian notions of lay participation, although the role of Emperor Sigismund (1410–1437) at the Council of Constance (1414–1418) in bringing the Great Schism to an end had given the old Caesaropapist tradition a revived honorific value. To such men as John Gerson (*c.* 1363–1429), the famous University Chancellor of Paris, the recourse to a Council was originally an emergency measure to end the otherwise insoluble scandal of the schism. Gerson appeals to the Aristotelean principle of 'equity' to justify the suspension of the usual machinery of Church government. He has in mind the universal canonistic opinion that summons by the Pope is a necessary precondition of a valid General Council. But what is to be done when it is uncertain which of several rival claimants is the rightful Pope and when in any case none will agree to summon a Council? Such a dilemma drove Gerson to the belief that Divine Providence must have in reserve some more reliable governing authority for the Church.

In his maturest Conciliar treatise, *De Potestate Ecclesiastica*, written during the Council of Constance, Gerson puts forward the claim that the Council possesses the supreme jurisdictional power of the Church to a full extent shared by no other ecclesiastical authority, not even the Pope. He bases this claim on the premise that the Council, as 'the assembling together and unified structure' of the Church, gives form (in the Aristotelean sense) to the corporate power potentially residing in the whole body of the faithful. Pope or Cardinals may err: but the Church and its representative Council remain

127

as the infallible repository of truth. Gerson does not intend to challenge the papal function as everyday executive head of the Church but he points out that the Papacy owes its jurisdictional power to its position in the hierarchical system of the *Sacerdotium* and can therefore be controlled by the corporate activity of the *Sacerdotium* working through the Council. The Pope's authority is a means towards the 'edification' or common good of the corporate organism of the Church. Ideally the Council should include the Pope, who is the highest in dignity of any single authority in the Church; but if he unreasonably tries to impede its activity it may proceed without him or even take steps to replace him.

Gerson's theory of representative government for the Church was confined to the clergy only. They alone have the right to vote in the deliberations of the Council, though he admits that 'any faithful person' may be heard in a consultative capacity in matters affecting the wellbeing of the Church. It is significant that when Gerson urges the Council's conformity to the requirements of Aristotle's mixed polity, he omits Aristotle's mention of democracy as an ingredient in this ideal mixture. For him indeed the presence of the laity is not necessary for they are represented in the Council by the clergy; the argument is reminiscent of the theory of 'virtual' representation of the voteless in the pre-1832 British House of Commons as put forward by those who opposed the reform of that institution.

This failure to draw the full logical consequence of his representative theories by claiming direct representation for every section of the faithful is a measure of the ambiguity inherent in the whole Conciliar position. It was still inseparably wedded to the orthodox hierarchical conception of authority as coming from above rather than below; this being the case, all the ingenuity of thinkers even of Gerson's calibre could not give the representative principle, based essentially on delegation from below, its full expression. Gerson's theory of 'virtual' representation fell between the two stools of complete

128

democratic control of the Church and the traditional monarchical government of the papacy. For the Pope also could
claim to be the *persona publica* 'virtually' representing the
community.

A Conciliar supporter of the next generation, Nicholas
of Cusa, in *De concordantia Catholica* (1434), tried to correct
the deficienciy in the older Conciliar viewpoint by arguing
that the authority of the sacerdotal hierarchy could be understood in a twofold sense. In one sense (its power of conferring
the Sacraments and of elucidating the meaning of revealed
truth) it comes from above, from Divine institution; but in a
second sense (its power of jurisdiction over its subjects) it
resembles all political institutions and follows the same rules
as they do. 'Since all men are by nature free', says Nicholas,
'it follows that every government, whether it rests its authority
on written law or on the living voice of the prince—derives
solely from the common agreement and consent of the subjects.' Political society arises from a pact among men to obey
their chosen rulers.

In this sense the Christian hierarchy itself depends on the
voluntary submission of the faithful for the purpose of their
salvation and Nicholas holds that it would be well that this
ultimate popular derivation of Church authority should be
emphasized in his own day by the revival of the primitive
practice of congregational election of bishops and priests.
Papal headship is not exempt from the general rule; it is
derivative 'from men and from the canons'. Canon Law is for
Nicholas the customary law of the Christian community,
based like all customary law on the principle of human consent
which is itself part of the Natural Law. Hence it is unlawful
for the Pope to claim a *plenitudo potestatis* over Canon Law;
in the ordinary administration of the Church he should act
with the advice of the Cardinals and may only change the law
with the sanction of a General Council.

Nicholas's attempt to reach an equitable distribution
of authority between the different parts of the Christian

129

organism is more carefully nuanced than that of the Conciliar theory of Gerson's generation. Indeed Nicholas's system is so far from being one of strict Conciliar predominance that one may almost question the usefulness of applying the term 'Conciliar' to it at all. The key to Nicholas's thought is the search for a principle of mutual harmony and consent (*concordantia*) which will link together all the members of the Christian body; the title of his book is the best indication of his aim.

The refinements to which Nicholas extends his theory in the desire to safeguard the due rights of all are ingenious. The Council, for example, may be below the Pope in one sense when it is a 'patriarchal' assembly, with the Pope presiding over the bishops; on the other hand, when its full representative capacity is in question, it is above the Pope, since its infallibility is less 'confused' than that of the Pope and is (or should be) unanimous. Nicholas makes a great point of the need for unanimity, carrying it as far as to say that Conciliar decisions may not bind particular provinces of the Church until explicitly accepted by them. In the same way papal rights are safeguarded by the statement that Conciliar decisions on matters of faith are not valid without papal consent. The Pope in his turn is warned not to override the jurisdictional rights of the episcopal hierarchy.

Despite all the subtleties of Nicholas's adjustments and the genuine passion for Church reform which burns beneath them, he, no more than Gerson, could achieve the impossible task of reconciliation between the hierarchical tradition of the medieval Church and the representative ideology. In the last resort he had to make his choice between them; he chose the papacy and ended his days as a Cardinal.

The case for the papacy's monarchical rule was put with a vigour equal to any on the Conciliar side by John of Torquemada (*d.* 1466) (not to be confused with the notorious Inquisitor!), a Spanish Dominican and a colleague of Cusa in the Sacred College. In his monumental *Summa de Ecclesia*

(1436) (written specifically against the claims of the Council of Basle (1431–1449)), Torquemada stated what he considered to be fundamental theological objections to the Conciliar position. More logical than the papalist thirteenth- and fourteenth-century canonist commentators, Torquemada denies the presupposition that the Church is a corporate body with the Council as its representative organ. It is primarily a collection of individuals each with an eternal destiny and it is to teach these the way of salvation that the Papacy exists. This being so, the Papacy's authority over the faithful must be essentially monarchical; otherwise it could not give the necessary infallible guidance. Torquemada adds the rather less convincing argument that, as the ideal form of government is recognized to be monarchy, it is that form by which the Church should be governed.

Torquemada's argument marks a bold departure from the corporatist ways of thinking which had been shown in the Conciliar period to possess such unsuspected dangers for papal authority. J. N. Figgis's dictum that Torquemada was 'the first exponent of the Divine Right of Kings' does not seem to contain much meaning, but it is true that Torquemada was reacting on behalf of the Papacy towards the Conciliar movement much as secular monarchs of the period were reacting against attempts of their own representative assemblies to curb their regalian rights.

The secular sovereigns had several theoretical weapons. One was the growing influence in favour of princely absolutism of a school of interpreters of Roman law. The so-called Reception of Roman law during the fifteenth century in the German homeland of Teutonic custom is a striking indication of the attraction of the principles of centralized government behind the Civil law for the new type of principality. The counterpart of the Reception in France is the new school of 'Humanist' commentators on the Civil law; they were interested in the original meaning of the *Corpus* in its classical context. Here too the result of their revival of the literal meaning of the

131

Roman sources was to reinforce the concentration of power in monarchical hands and hence to play a part in the eclipse of the medieval representative idea. In practice this eclipse is reflected in the progressive infrequency of the meetings of representative assemblies on the Continent from the sixteenth century onwards. England alone preserved more continuity with the medieval past in this respect, owing to her monarchy's traditional policy of establishing its central power by careful association with the representative assemblies of its realm rather than by neglect. Parliaments were often packed, browbeaten or manipulated by the Crown; but they remained an indispensable part of the Crown's machinery of government.

If representation was going generally out of favour as the Middle Ages drew to their close, it would be inaccurate to say that a full-blown theory of monarchical absolutism had yet taken its place. Isolated thinkers such as Aeneas Sylvius Piccolomini (1405–1464), later Pope Pius II, might uphold the theory of imperial irresponsibility to the law, even if the Emperor acts unjustly. But on the whole the monarchs of the time preferred to emphasize the more traditional appeal to their 'regalian rights' which they declared to be inalienable.

The third great issue in this age of ambiguity is the progressive snapping of the close connection between *Sacerdotium* and *Regnum*. The transformation of the latter into the State with its own autonomous functions was the logical outcome of the rediscovery of Roman law and Aristotle as well as of the economic and political changes brought about by the rise of a literate, wealthy and administratively competent laity. The ages of clerical monopoly of the administrative and intellectual worlds had passed and with their passing the close political links between the secular government and the ecclesiastical hierarchy tended to weaken.

The eclipse of the old Caesaro-papist ideal of the Emperor as the moderator of Christendom was a sign of the changing times. Dante tried to give it a more universal basis than it had

ever possessed in fact or theory and after him the less ambitious Ockham still toyed with the idea of the Emperor's
right to interfere in case of emergency with the internal affairs
of the *Sacerdotium* if the Pope failed to do his duty; like John
of Paris, from whom he may derive the idea, Ockham grants
to the Papacy the right on the same terms to interfere with
the *Regnum*. Even in the fifteenth century Nicholas of Cusa
still clings to the old idea of harmoniously co-operative
authorities in the Christian Commonwealth. But the possi-
bilities of achieving this dream had long since gone and the
Papacy itself had been the first to realize the fact.

One of the features of fifteenth-century diplomacy is
the settlement of outstanding ecclesiastical issues in the
various countries of western Europe by bilateral agreements
concluded between the Papacy and the respective national
monarchies. The so-called Concordats of 1418 between
the reunited Papacy under Martin V (1417–1431) and the
'nations' present at the Council of Constance is one instance
of the process. Others are the Concordat of Vienna in 1448
between Frederick III of Austria (1440–1493) and Pope
Nicholas V (1447–1455), and the Concordat of Bologna in
1516 between Francis I of France (1515–1547) and Pope Leo X
(1513–1521). In all these agreements the secular sovereigns
take up an almost independent position *vis-à-vis* the Papacy.
The Concordats give the impression of being negotiations
between equal sovereign powers rather than arrangements
between the head of the Church and his spiritual sons.

This practical development led on the theoretical plane
to the decline of the conception of the Papacy's direct temporal power which now became something of an embarrass-
ment to papal political action. The credit for the first explicit
rejection of the hierocratic theory by a prominent papal
apologist must be given to Torquemada, who here appears
once more as a specimen of the enlightened conservatism
which is ready for ruthless sacrifice of an outmoded position
for the sake of the institution which it has served. Torquemada

is usually described as the originator of the modern Catholic theory of the 'indirect' power of the Papacy in temporal affairs. The term 'indirect power' does not as a matter of fact occur in his work, but Torquemada's definition of the scope of papal authority in temporal matters does correspond broadly to the intention of Bellarmine (1542–1621) and other formulators of the later specific theory of indirect power.

The Papacy, declares Torquemada in his *Summa de Ecclesia*, has the right to such temporal power as is necessary 'for the preservation of religion, the guidance of the faithful to eternal salvation, the punishment of sins and the preservation of peace among Christian people'. In many ways the definition is reminiscent of Innocent III's claim to intervene in temporal affairs *pro ratione peccati*; Torquemada indeed cites Innocent explicitly in corroboration of his own argument.

Like Innocent, Torquemada deduces from the indirect powers rather more sweeping consequences than modern Catholic advocates of the indirect power theory would perhaps care to admit. According to him, the Pope may 'give laws' to secular monarchs by virtue of the higher end which is the concern of his office; he may depose monarchs who failed in their duty and may absolve the subjects of excommunicated monarchs from their oaths of allegiance (the example of Gregory VII is cited by Torquemada). The Pope may also call for the use of force to suppress heresy or in the case of a just war; he may deprive infidel or apostate rulers of their dominion over the faithful (though Torquemada admits that the dominion of infidels is in itself lawful and just) and may supplement justice when it fails. We even find Torquemada echoing long-outdated claims on behalf of the Papacy to translate the Empire and to exercise rule during an imperial vacancy. His more usual attitude, however, is to leave aside the anachronistic conflict with the Empire and to concentrate on the more real problem of the Papacy's relations with the national monarchies. He is certainly not to be reckoned as an advocate of secular autonomy from any control by the Papacy; but his

134

work does mark the abandonment of the hierocratic claims to papal *plenitudo potestatis* in temporal affairs which had played so large a part in the history of the thirteenth and fourteenth centuries.

Torquemada and the Papacy, for which he fought, still naturally thought in terms of an inseparable connection between Church and State. So did all writers on politics during the period; even a sceptic like Machiavelli (1469–1527) still favours an established religion as a buttress for the political framework and in so doing looks back, consciously or unconsciously, to Marsiglio. But the mention of Machiavelli reminds us of a tendency of which he is the most elaborate and famous exponent, but which was already present before his time. This was the tendency to separate ethics from politics, to assume that politics possessed a set of laws of its own which need not coincide with those of ordinary morality.

We are all familiar with Machiavelli's doctrine of *raison d'état*, the justifying of even an immoral means to achieve a political end, and we are aware that the cynical maxims of *The Prince* are merely the explicit statement of the habitual political practice of Renaissance Italy. It is not so well known that the *raison d'état* doctrine had medieval antecedents; the idea that the sovereign can take extraordinary emergency measures for the common good is a step on the way to Machiavellianism. So is the idea current in some exasperated ecclesiastical circles during the Great Schism that any measures, even the most violent, might be taken to achieve the reunion of the Church. Thus Dietrich of Niem (*c.* 1340–1418) speaks in his *De Modis uniendi et reformandi ecclesiam in Concilio Universali* of the lawfulness of imprisoning or even executing the Pope if he stands in the way of a settlement of the Schism.

This *raison d'Eglise* (if it may so be called) has probable associations with the contemporary apologies for tyrannicide such as that by Jean Petit (1360?–1411), the Parisian academic who defended the assassination of the Duke of Orleans in 1407 on the ground that he was a tyrant and a menace to the common good. This view in its turn would receive support from the revived study of Greek and Roman history undertaken by Renaissance humanism. We can see the change in graphic illustration by comparing the presentation of Brutus, the murderer of Julius Caesar, by two great poets. The treason of Dante's Brutus has placed him in the lowest depths of the *Inferno*; but the participation of Shakespeare's Brutus, 'the noblest Roman of them all', in Caesar's murder was

'. . . only in a general honest thought,
And common good to all . . .'

It is hard to know where to bring to an end a general sketch of the political thought of the Middle Ages. Some of its greatest institutions, the Catholic Church, the representative system, ecclesiastical and secular law, are still with us and still exercise a potent influence in ways which medieval minds could not have suspected. Yet a break in continuity occurred somewhere in the age of ambiguity with which this sketch must close; by the end of that period the fundamental medieval political idea of a Christian Commonwealth with its coordinated secular and religious branches had departed. Perhaps, like every individual man, it had been dying from the moment of its birth; much of this book has been occupied with tracing the vicissitudes of its passage to the grave. The disintegration of the Christian social and political *Respublica* was in progress long before the Reformation. Yet the explicitly accepted religious fragmentation of western Christendom in the sixteenth century was the final proclamation that the old ideal was dead and with it the medieval world.

BIBLIOGRAPHY

I. FOR GENERAL READING

(Works in this section have been selected with the intention of providing some suggestions for readers interested in following up the general themes dealt with in this book.)

MCILWAIN, C. H. : *The growth of political thought in the West from the Greeks to the end of the Middle Ages* (New York, 1932) traces European speculation on politics from its beginnings in classical times to the transition from medieval to modern thought at the close of the fifteenth century. The main theme of the book is the combination of Graeco-Roman, Germanic and Christian concepts by medieval tradition to bring about a society in which central government was limited, not by specific constitutional checks, but by rights conceived as belonging in general and in particular to the members of the community.

CARLYLE, R. W. and A. J.: *Mediaeval political theory in the West* (6 vols., London, 1903–36) is specially valuable for the large number of verbatim quotations from primary sources in their original languages. In general the earlier Middle Ages (up to the thirteenth century) are treated more satisfactorily than are the fourteenth and fifteenth centuries, which are dealt with more sketchily. The six volumes deal respectively with: (i) classical and early Christian thought; (ii) the Canonists and Civilians; (iii) feudal and Germanic ideas; (iv) the Investiture Contest; (v) the thirteenth century; (vi) the fourteenth, fifteenth and sixteenth centuries.

GIERKE, O.: *Political Theories of the Middle Age* (an extract translated by Maitland, F. W., Cambridge, 1900, from the author's *Das deutsche Genossenschaftsrecht*) has as its main thesis that the men of the Middle Ages did not follow up the logical implications of their own political thought. Gierke holds that this thought, embodied in the ideals of unity and organic arrangement of society, necessarily implies the concept

137

of 'group-personality'. He attributes the failure to evolve such a concept to the intrusion of what he describes as 'antique-modern' conceptions of politics, which tended to regard all legal entities other than the State and the individual as 'fictitious'. Gierke regards the civilians and still more the canonists as responsible for the consequent 'atomization' in political thought of the social and political community. Maitland's introduction to his translation is a characteristically brilliant exposition for English readers of Gierke's theory.

LEWIS, E.: 'Organic tendencies in mediaeval political thought' in *American Political Science Review*, 1938, is an example of the stringent criticism to which Gierke's outlook has been subjected in recent years.

TROELTSCH, E.: *The social teaching of the Christian Churches* (English translation, 2 vols., London, 1931) is also written to prove a thesis. Troeltsch maintains that primitive and Patristic Christianity, having no interest outside the spiritual life of its own fellowship, took no trouble to work out a political philosophy, but contented itself with taking over the already existing classical concepts, such as the Law of Nature (understood in a relative sense owing to human sin) and a past golden age of Mankind. Medieval Catholicism, on the other hand, forced by circumstances into more intimate contact with civil society, sought to control the whole of social life. In practice however the Church made little change in the classical idea of Natural Law, upon which it superimposed the sanctions and graces of revealed religion. Thus there was no attempt in the Middle Ages to create a distinctively Christian social or political ethic; the Church was content to act as the interpreter and enforcer of rational Natural Law. The chief share in the dissolution of the medieval order was, Troeltsch thinks, taken by the 'sects', the less organized and more individualistic elements in Christianity.

CRUMP, C. G., and JACOB, E. F. (edited), *The legacy of the Middle Ages* (Oxford, 1926) contains some helpful essays. Powicke, F. M., 'Christian life in the Middle Ages', comments on the penetration of an at least nominal Christianity at all levels of the social structure. Le Bras, G., 'Canon Law' is a good short introduction to the history and importance of the *Corpus Iuris Canonici*. Jacob, E. F., 'Political thought', sees the Middle Ages as transmitting two main political concepts; on the one hand, the unitary conception of the State, derived from antiquity, and on the other, a pluralistic view of political society.

138

POWICKE, F. M.: 'Reflections on the Medieval State' in *Transactions of the Royal Historical Society*, 1936, and reprinted in his *Ways of Medieval life and Thought* (London, 1949), surveys the problems involved in the use of the concept and of other medieval political terms.

KERN, F.: *Kingship and law in the Middle Ages* (English translation, Oxford, 1939) is a convenient account of Germanic legal and customary concepts. Kern emphasizes the function of law as a guarantee of certain inviolable rights to all who shared in it, and of kingship as the chief agency to enunciate and enforce this law.

ARQUILLIÈRE, H. X.: *L'augustinisme politique* (2nd edition, Paris, 1955) argues that St. Augustine's emphasis on the lack of justice in a non-Christian State was misunderstood in the Dark Ages. He believes that this bastard political Augustinism led to the conception that all secular power must be visibly associated with the Church to be truly capable of fulfilling its function. In his *Saint Grégoire VII* (Paris, 1934) Arquillière traces a further development and claims to show, by study of the writers, official and unofficial, on both sides during the Investiture Contest, that by the eleventh century both *Sacerdotium* and *Regnum* had accepted as axiomatic the concept of a single interdependent Christian society. The point at issue in Gregory's time was whether this society should be ruled by Caesaro-papism or by Papal theocracy.

ULLMANN, W.: *Medieval Papalism* (London, 1949) contends that the main medieval Canonist tradition supported the theory of direct papal power in temporal affairs. With this should be compared a review of Ullmann's book by Stickler, A. M., under the title 'Concerning the political theories of the medieval Canonists' in *Traditio*, 1951, in which Ullmann's interpretation is strongly criticized as onesided. In a later book, *The growth of Papal government in the Middle Ages* (London, 1955), Ullmann attempts to trace the hierocratic Papalist ideology of later medieval times back into the Dark Ages and even the Patristic period. His most striking contention is that a theory of dualism in the relationship of the early medieval Church and the secular power was the exception rather than the rule. The Gelasian theory itself was not an assertion of dualism but a claim for the Papacy of monistic supremacy, even in the temporal sphere. The theme of the whole book is the conflict between this claim and the rival Caesaro-papist claim of the secular Christian authority. Ullmann ends his survey on the eve of what he would

139

regard as the codification of the hierocratic theory by Canonist tradition after Gratian.

Two articles in the collection *Sacerdozio e Regno da Gregorio VII a Bonifacio VIII* (Rome, 1954) should be mentioned. Stickler, A. M., 'Sacerdozio e Regno nelle nuove richerche attorno ai secoli XII e XIII nei Decretisti e Decretalisti di Gregorio IX', contends that the main position of the canonists of the period · before Gregory IX was still traditional dualism and that hierocratic theories arose later as a result of a confusion over the nature of the coercive material power of the Church. Maccarone, M., *Potestas directa e Potestas indirecta* nei teologi del XII e XIII secolo', believes that the theory of direct power did not appear among theologians until the thirteenth century.

TIERNEY, B.: *Foundations of the Conciliar theory* (Cambridge, 1955) provides a well-documented account of the development of Canonistic views on the internal structure of the Church and shows how they prepared the way for the Conciliar movement of the fifteenth century. He gives particular emphasis to the importance of the corporation theory as worked out by the Decretalists of the thirteenth and fourteenth centuries. The same writer's 'Some recent works on the political theories of the medieval Canonists' in *Traditio*, 1954, supplies a handy and impartially critical survey of recent scholarship and differences of opinion.

POST, G.: '*Plena potestas* and consent in medieval assemblies' in *Traditio*, 1943, shows the dependence of representative theories on the techniques of proctorial representation evolved in Civil and Canon Law, while the same writer's 'Roman Law and early representation in Spain and Italy' in *Speculum*, 1943, concludes that Italian *milieux* were the pioneers in the development of representative practice.

LAGARDE, G.: *La naissance de l'ésprit laïque au déclin du moyen age* (6 vols., St. Paul-trois-Chateaux, 1934–46) gives a stimulating survey of the cross-currents of political and social theory in the thirteenth and fourteenth centuries, though its desire to trace modern secularism back into the medieval period leads to a certain loss of historical perspective. Vol. III ('Secteur social de la Scolastique') contains useful material on the impact of Aristotle's *Politics* on thirteenth-century thought. The same volume contains a good outline of St. Thomas Aquinas's political views.

AUBERT, J. M.: *Le droit Romain dans l'oeuvre de St. Thomas* (Paris, 1955) despite the limitation in scope suggested by its title, is in fact a reliable guide to the whole subject of St. Thomas's philosophy of law, the key to the saint's political thought.

RIVIÈRE, J.: *Le problème de l'Eglise et de l'Etat au temps de Philippe le Bel* (Paris, 1926) opens with an account of the development of the theory of Papal direct temporal power, which it traces back to Gregorian times and the twelfth century. The book treats in detail the official and publicistic arguments on both sides during the Bonifacian controversy, paying particular attention to Giles of Rome, James of Viterbo and John of Paris.

GWYNN, A.: *The English Austin Friars* (Oxford, 1940) gives detailed attention in the first part of his book to the Augustinian controversialists and explains the various vicissitudes through which Giles's *dominium* theory passed before it reached Wycliffe.

The following entries refer to Dante, Marsiglio, Ockham and the Conciliar movement:

GILSON, E.: *Dante the philosopher* (English translation, London, 1948) contains a brilliantly written interpretation of Dante's vision of world order. According to Gilson, Dante was no systematic philosopher but used a variety of sources to elaborate his plea for a universal Empire, enjoying complete independence and directing Man to a specifically temporal end.

D'ENTRÈVES, A. P.: *Dante as a political thinker* (Oxford, 1952) describes the evolution of Dante's political thought in three phases, symbolized by the concepts *Civitas*, *Imperium* and *Ecclesia*. He believes that Roman Law was the most important factor in Dante's adoption of the Imperial concept. d'Entrèves sees in the ideas of the *Convivio* a curious mixture of the Aristotelean 'natural' view and the 'conventional' view of St. Augustine with regard to political authority. *The Divine Comedy* is interpreted as an abandonment of the *Monarchia*'s ideal of universal temporal order in favour of a more spiritualized conception of moral regeneration through the Church.

PREVITÉ-ORTON, C. W.: 'Marsilius of Padua' in *Proceedings of the British Academy*, 1935, is a short introduction to Marsiglio's thought. It emphasizes the influence of the political practice of contemporary Italian city-states on Marsiglio's theories.

LAGARDE, op. cit., Vol. II, gives a lively but partisan presentation of Marsiglio as an anticipator of the modern totalitarian State, particularly in his claim for the omnicompetence of secular authority, even in the religious field.

GEWIRTH, A.: *Marsilius of Padua*, vol. i (New York, 1951) the only full-scale English treatment, believes that Marsiglio's idea of the State embodies genuine democratic elements and that Marsiglio's community retains a right of ultimate control over the *pars principans*. Gewirth holds that the Marsilian dissociation of politics from ethics was assisted partly by an emphasis on the biological rather than the teleological aspects of Aristotle's approach and partly from the utilization of St. Augustine's political pessimism.

LAGARDE, op. cit., vols. iv-vi, discusses in detail the intellectual and material background to Ockham's theories on law and politics. He believes that Ockham's political Nominalism, with its refusal to see reality outside individuals, paved the way for the atomization of the medieval political community. Tierney, *Foundations* (p. 100), points out that Lagarde's view seems to be essentially a revival of Gierke's antithesis between organic and atomistic theories in the Middle Ages, with Ockham taking the place of the Canonists as the agent of disintegration. Lagarde's views are discussed and criticized by Morrall, J. B., 'Some notes on a recent interpretation of William of Ockham's political philosophy' in *Franciscan Studies*, 1949.

JEDIN, H.: *A History of the Council of Trent*, vol. i (English translation, London, 1957) contains in its first book ('Council and reform from the Council of Basle to the Lateran Council') a remarkable survey of Conciliarist and Papalist thought on Church government over the whole of the fifteenth century. The influence of Torquemada as spokesman for the revived monarchical power is stressed. Jedin also emphasizes the considerable extent to which Conciliarist ideas survived even after the victory of the Papacy over the Council of Basle.

JACOB, E. F.: *Essays in the Conciliar Epoch* (2nd edition, Manchester, 1952) includes a useful essay on 'Conciliar thought' (especially noteworthy for its analysis of Gerson's conception of Church government) and an interpretation of 'Ockham as a political thinker'. The same writer's 'Nicholas of Cusa' in Hearnshaw, F. J. C. (edited), *The social and political ideas of some thinkers of the Renaissance and Reformation* (London, 1925), is a good introduction to this interesting thinker, whose *De Concordantia Catholica* is summarized and described.

II. FOR SPECIALIZED STUDY

BERNHEIM, E.: *Mittelalterliche Zeitanschauung in ihrem Einfluss auf Politik und Geschichtsschreibung.* (Tubingen, 1918.)

CALASSO, F.: *I Glossatori e la teoria della sovranità.* (2nd edition. Milan, 1950.)

COVILLE, A.: *Jean Petit: la question du tyrannicide au commencement du XVe siècle.* (Paris, 1932.)

FIGGIS, J. N.: *From Gerson to Grotius.* (Cambridge, 1907.)

FIGGIS, J. N.: *The Divine right of kings.* (2nd edition, Cambridge, 1914.)

FLICHE, A.: *La réforme Grégorienne.* (3 vols., Paris, 1924–37.)

FOLZ, R.: *L'idée d'Empire en Occident du Ve au XIVe siècle.* (Paris, 1953.)

GEWIRTH, A.: 'John of Jandun and the *Defensor Pacis,* in *Speculum.* (1948.)

GILBY, T.: *Principality and polity: Aquinas and the rise of State theory in the West.* (London, 1958.)

GRABMANN, M.: *Studien über den Einfluss der aristotelischen Philosophie auf die mittelalterlichen Theorien über der Verhältnis von Kirche und Staat.* (Munich, 1934.)

KANTOROWICZ, E.: *'Pro Patria Mori* in medieval political thought' in *American Historical Review.* (1951.)

KANTOROWICZ, E.: *The King's two bodies; a study in medieval political thought.* (Princeton, 1957.)

LACHANCE, L.: *L'humanisme politique de St. Thomas.* (2 vols., Paris–Montreal, 1941.)

LECLERCQ, J.: *Jean de Paris et l'écclesiologie du XIIIe siècle.* (Paris, 1942.)

MACCARONE, M.: *Chiesa e stato nella dottrina di Papa Innocenzo III.* (Rome, 1940.)

MACCARONE, M.: *Vicarius Christi:* Storia del titolo papale. (Rome, 1952.)

MARIANI, U.: *Scrittori politici Agostiniani del secolo XIV.* (Florence, 1927.)

MARTIN, C.: 'Some medieval commentaries on Aristotle's *Politics'* in *History.* (1951.)

MARTIN, V.: *Les origines du Gallicanisme.* (2 vols., Paris, 1939.)

MOCHI ONORY, S.: *Fonti canonistiche dell' idea moderna dello Stato.* (Milan, 1951.)

143

POST, G.: 'Two notes on Nationalism in the Middle Ages' in *Traditio*. (1953.)

RUPP, J.: *L'idée de chrétienté dans la pensée pontificale des origines à Innocent III*. (Paris, 1939.)

SCHOLZ, R.: *Wilhelm von Ockham als politischer denker*. (Stuttgart, 1944.)

ULLMANN, W.: 'The development of the medieval idea of sovereignty' in *English Historical Review*. (1949.)

WATT, J.: 'The early medieval Canonists and the formation of Conciliar theory' in *Irish Theological Quarterly*. (1957.)

III. ON THE MEDIEVAL BACKGROUND

BLOCH, M.: *La société féodale*. (2 vols., Paris, 1949.)

CRUMP, C. G., and JACOB, E. F.: *The legacy of the Middle Ages*. (Oxford, 1926.)

FLICHE, A., and MARTIN, V. (edited): *Histoire de l'Eglise*. (Paris, 1934ff.)

GANSHOF, F. L.: *Feudalism*. (English translation, London, 1952.)

GILSON, E.: *Christian philosophy in the Middle Ages*. (London, 1955.)

GILSON, E.: *Introduction à l'étude de St. Augustin*. (Paris, 1929.)

LE GOFF, J.: *Les intellectuels du moyen âge*. (Paris, 1957.)

MARROU, H.: *St. Augustine and Augustinism*. (English translation, London, 1957.)

PERROY, E. (edited): *Le moyen âge*. (Paris, 1955.)

POOLE, R. L.: *Illustrations of medieval thought and learning*. (2nd edition, London, 1920.)

RASHDALL, H.: *The medieval universities*. (Revised edition, edited by Powicke, F. M., and Emden, A. B., 3 vols., Oxford, 1936.)

SOUTHERN, R.: *The making of the Middle Ages*. (London, 1953.)

VIGNAUX, P.: *La pensée au moyen âge*. (Paris, 1948.)

IV. EDITIONS AND TRANSLATIONS OF PRIMARY SOURCES

(a) Collections and Anthologies

EHLER, S. Z., and MORRALL, J. B.: Church and State through the centuries. (Translated official documents, London, 1954.)

FRIEDBERG, E.: *Corpus Iuris Canonici*. (2 vols, Leipzig, 1879–81.)

KRUEGER, P., and MOMMSEN, T.: *Corpus Iuris Civili.* (3 vols., Berlin, 1928.)

LEWIS, E.: *Medieval Political ideas.* (Translated extracts, 2 vols., London, 1954.)

LO GRASSO, J. B.: *Ecclesia et Status.* (Anthology in original languages, 2nd edition, Rome, 1952.)

MIGNE, J. P.: *Patrologia Latina.* (Paris, 1844 ff.)

(*b*) *Individual writers*

ARISTOTLE: *Politics.* (Latin translation by William of Moerbeke, edited by Susemihl, F., Leipzig, 1872.)

BEAUMANOIR: *Coutumes de Beauvaisis.* (Edited by Salmon, A, 2 vols, Paris, 1899–1900.)

BRACTON: *De legibus et consuetudinibus Angliae.* (Edited by Woodbine, G., 4 vols, New Haven, 1915–42.)

DANTE: *Convivio.* (English translation by Wicksteed, P. H., London, 1903.)

DANTE: *De Monarchia.* (Edited by Vinay, P., Florence, 1950.)

DANTE: *Monarchy.* (English translation by Nicol, D., London, 1954.)

DANTE: *Opera omnia.* (Edited by Toynbee, P., 4th edition., Oxford, 1924.)

FORTESCUE, SIR JOHN: *De laudibus legum Angliae.* (Edited by Chrimes, S. B., London, 1942.)

GERSON: *Opera omnia.* (Edited by Du Pin, E., 5 vols., Antwerp, 1706.)

GILES OF ROME: *De potestate ecclesiastica.* (Edited by Scholz, R., Weimar, 1929.)

JAMES OF VITERBO: *De regimine Christiano.* (Edited by Arquillière, H. X., Paris, 1926.)

JOHN OF PARIS: *De potestate regia et papali.* (Edited by Leclercq, J., in op. cit., Paris, 1942.)

JOHN OF SALISBURY: *Policraticus.* (Edited by Webb, C. C. J., Oxford, 1909.)

JOHN OF SALISBURY: *The Statesman's Book.* (Translation of *Policraticus* by Dickinson, J., New York, 1927.)

MARSIGLIO OF PADUA: *Defensor Pacis.* (Edited by Previté-Orton, C. W., Cambridge, 1928.)

MARSIGLIO OF PADUA: *The Defender of Peace.* (English translation of *Defensor Pacis* by Gewirth, A., in vol. ii of op. cit., New York, 1956.)

NICHOLAS OF CUSA: *Opera omnia.* (Basle, 1565.)

BIBLIOGRAPHY

THOMAS AQUINAS, ST.: *Selected political writings.* (Edited by d'Entrèves, A. P., with English translation by Dawson, J. G., Oxford, 1948.)

TORQUEMADA: *Summa de Ecclesia.* (Rome, 1489.)

WILLIAM OF OCKHAM: *Opera politica.* (Manchester, 1940 ff.)

WILLIAM OF OCKHAM: *Breviloquium.* (Edited by Scholz, R., in op. cit., Stuttgart, 1944.)

WYCLIFFE, JOHN: *De dominio Divino.* (Edited by Poole, R. L., London, 1890.)

WYCLIFFE, JOHN: *De officio regis.* (Edited by Pollard, A. W., and Sayle, C., London, 1887.)

INDEX OF PERSONAL NAMES

INDEX OF SUBJECTS